Kelly Lee–Creel and Rebecca Söder

HANDMADE HOSTESS

12 Imaginative Party Ideas for Unforgettable Entertaining

37 Sewing & Craft Projects • 12 Desserts

stashBOOKS®

an imprint of C&T Publishing

Text and Artwork copyright © 2013 by Kelly Lee-Creel

Recipe text copyright © 2013 by Rebecca Söder

Photography copyright © 2013 by Kekoa Lee-Creel

Publisher: Amy Marson

Creative Director: Gailen Runge

Art Director / Book Designer: Kristy Zacharias

Editor: Cynthia Bix

Technical Editors: Ann Haley and Gailen Runge

Page Layout Artist: Kerry Graham

Production Coordinator: Jenny Davis

Production Editor: Alice Mace Nakanishi

Illustrators: Kelly Lee-Creel and Valyrie Friedman

Photographer: Kekoa Lee-Creel

Published by Stash Books, an imprint of C&T Publishing, Inc., P.O. Box 1456, Lafayette, CA 94549

Library of Congress Cataloging-in-Publication Data

Lee-Creel, Kelly, 1980-

 Handmade hostess : 12 imaginative party ideas for unforgettable entertaining - 37 sewing & craft projects - 12 desserts / Kelly Lee-Creel and Rebecca Söder.

   pages cm

 ISBN 978-1-60705-560-0 (soft cover)

 1. Party decorations. 2. Sewing. 3. Textile crafts. 4. Desserts. I. Söder, Rebecca, 1984- II. Title.

 TT900.P3L45 2013

 646.2--dc23

                2012026278

Printed in China

10 9 8 7 6 5 4 3 2 1

DEDICATION

For Mom and Dad,

Kekoa and Jordan,

Taylor and Kaden

CONTENTS

FOREWORD

This book is a love letter.

Here we have tried to capture the heart of our family gatherings and special occasions—the way we care for one another through sewing, decorating, and baking, and the great lengths we go to in order to recapture some of our very best childhood memories, which always seem to have happened around the holidays.

However, in the end, this book is the love letter our families wrote back to us. They gathered alongside us to usher this book into existence, carrying us along during the hard parts and contributing their own gifts, without which we could not have made it.

We are also grateful to our friends, both old and new, who opened their homes to us. Lastly, we are thankful to you, the reader. This is our way of throwing open the door and welcoming you to the party. We hope these words and images inspire you and help you shower your own special people with love.

—*Kelly and Rebecca*

HANDMADE HOSTESS PRIMER

Having people over for a special event can be a wonderful thrill. The bustle of getting ready, cleaning house, and pulling out the fine dishes gets our hearts beating fast. Our imaginations run wild with ideas for making the party unique, and soon we're off to the fabric store or the baking aisle to gather up supplies.

We believe that making *something* special is an opportunity to make *someone* feel special. The best entertainers remember two key things—attention to the personal touches that make your guests feel welcome, and at least one over-the-top showstopper that makes the event memorable. This book will teach you to fearlessly blend the simple with the extravagant.

An Eye on the Basics

Beautiful, creative decorations add so much to a party, but remember that an incredible soiree is only incredible if your guests have a warm greeting; a comfy place to sit; and easy access to the things they need, such as napkins, drinks, and restrooms.

We have sometimes made the mistake of focusing so much on the food and decorations that by the time our guests arrived, we were harried, stressed-out hosts. We waved our arriving friends haphazardly toward the living room while we rushed back to the kitchen— or even worse, to the sewing machine, where stacks of napkins were waiting to be hemmed. Our unsuspecting family members found themselves enlisted to help wrap up the rest of our incomplete projects. If we had used The Checklist (below), we might have avoided this problem.

So, finish the basics on this list first. Once The Checklist is complete, you are free to lavish the event with your creativity.

The Checklist

✓ Seating

✓ Tables

✓ Table linens

✓ Beverages

✓ Dishes and flatware

✓ Place cards and seating assignments

✓ Personal touches and party favors

✓ Accessibility

Seating Whenever possible, try to ensure that every guest has a seat, even if that means renting additional chairs, mixing in extras from your patio, or reserving picnic tables at the park. Consider using floor pillows or blankets for small children.

Tables How many tables do you need? Will your dining table work, or do you need to borrow a folding table? Will there be a separate buffet or a place for birthday presents? Gift tables should be within sight of the arrival area so guests have their hands free. Station food and drinks where you would like guests to mingle. This is a great way to lure the party to the living room or outside.

Table linens This book is full of ideas for custom tablecloths, napkins, and napkin rings. If you are planning a large party, you may find it more cost effective to rent some of the table linens (or make very basic ones in reusable colors such as white) and then mix in your custom designs. When budget is an issue at a large event, we like to make one table the focal point—such as an elegant dessert bar—and leave the other tables simple and understated.

Beverages Will guests serve themselves? Do you have the necessary items, such as pitchers, drink dispensers, cups, and straws? Is there a place to recycle glass bottles or cans? If you are planning to serve hot tea or coffee, will you need extra cups and items like cream and sugar? If guests are freely moving about your home, you may want to keep in mind that children, fruit punch, and carpets do not mix well.

Dishes and flatware Whether you are serving hors d'oeuvres, hot dogs, or a multicourse meal, decide if you are going to use paper plates or your best china. If you are using your own dishes, have a plan for clearing the table and storing used items (in a plastic bin hidden in the laundry room, for example) until they can be rinsed and loaded into the dishwasher after the event is over.

Place cards and seating assignments We love place cards and use them liberally—even at small family gatherings. While you are arranging seats, consider the flow of the event. Is it clear where guests should go? At an intimate dinner, you may want to set younger children up at a separate table with their own décor. Preteens and teens will thank you for including them with guests their own age—or better yet, the adults.

Personal touches and party favors A celebration can be a wonderful gift to your guests, and nowhere is this more evident than in the party favors. Where you can, show that you care. Sometimes this means writing a note that says "Glad you are here" and slipping it next to the person's napkin. A thoughtful hostess pays attention to details; she includes a special little touch such as a lemon wedge in guests' water.

Accessibility Don't forget to consider things like parking, availability of restrooms, and any guests with special needs.

The Schedule

After you have worked your way through The Checklist (page 6), make a shopping list of additional items you may need, such as chairs, place settings, and supplies. Determine a rough schedule for the party preparations and the event itself. Note when you will need to heat food, cut the cake, or start a game.

Now is a good time to do a walk-through. Pretend you are a guest arriving at the party. Which items will need to be rearranged, cleaned, or repaired so that the party has a nice flow?

If you have chosen to use dishes or table linens you already own, try setting up a vignette on the table to see how things look together. As you purchase supplies, test the items out together so you can develop a color story and style.

Whenever possible, try to set up as many of the decorations as possible *in advance* (not the morning of). Most of us underestimate how long things may take, and nothing is worse than having guests arrive while you are still trying to set up.

The night before the party, do a last-minute sanity check. Are there any items on your to-do list that should be crossed off? Look over the list of basics again. The most important element of the party is the comfort of your friends and family. Give yourself permission to save a project for next time.

Lastly, if the party is in your home, we recommend doing any deep cleaning at least a week before the party and a light touch-up the day before the event. When you are hosting the party somewhere else, try to visit the location ahead of time and take any necessary measurements. Snap a few photographs to help you plan for setup.

The day of the party, you should *not*:

- start a new sewing project (unless it is one you have made before and you are very skilled),

- run to the grocery store so you can add an extra menu item,

- assemble the party favors or make the center-piece, or

- undertake spring cleaning tasks you have been putting off for the better part of a year!

Great Expectations: How to Avoid Being a Stressed-Out Hostess

We don't do it all, and neither should you (unless you really, really want to). The only good reason to do any of this—the decorating and celebrating, baking and making—is because you want to, and doing it yourself will give you immense satisfaction. There are lots of reasons we get caught up in trying to entertain our friends and families, but the best celebrations, however simple, are the ones that come from the heart.

To Make or Buy

Sometimes you are running short on time. It is perfectly acceptable to buy something even if you know you could have made it yourself. Create the things you enjoy making. Let the rest go.

Many times our most festive parties are only for our very closest friends and family. We encourage you to think about ways that you could scale up or down the recipes and ideas in this book to fit your own circle—no matter how large or small.

About the Projects

The sewing projects vary in difficulty from extremely easy to advanced. If you are new to sewing, we encourage you to try your hand at the basic tablecloth patterns in Special Techniques (page 153), or a simple project such as the Pixie Dust Pouch (page 77). However, even some of the more challenging patterns are suitable for beginners, since many of the shapes are organic and designed to be decorative, not functional.

Materials and Supplies

Throughout this book, we recommend various supplies. These are the ones we use the most.

Bodkin This little tool has a large eye like a needle but a blunt end instead of a point. Use it to thread ribbon through a channel stitched in fabric, as in the ruched corners of the End of the Rainbow Tablecloth (page 44).

Freezer paper Available in most grocery stores, freezer paper is like waxed paper with the wax on only one side. A hot iron will temporarily adhere freezer paper to fabric, making it a great pattern template material. Not only that, but it's also useful in some of our baking recipes!

Hot glue gun This indispensable crafter's tool is used in many of our projects. It gets very hot; use it with care!

Interfacing Using the right interfacing for your project will make a big difference, such as the Pellon Decor-Bond for the Fabric Flowers (page 52). Special requirements and our recommendations are noted with each project. When using heavy-duty interfacing, such as in the Santa's Sleigh Centerpiece (page 14), we recommend using one such as Pellon Peltex 70 Ultra-Firm Stabilizer and cutting it *without* seam allowances. Then, fuse a featherweight fusible interfacing (such as Pellon 911FF Fusible Featherweight) over the Peltex 70 and into the seams. This requires additional prep work and cutting, but it helps provide shape to the project while eliminating bulk in the seams.

Special fabrics We enjoy experimenting with special fabrics like silks, velvet, linens, and tulle. The most important thing is to get the right needle, thread, and tension combo and then to have fun with it. For advice on handling specific fabrics, see Special Techniques (page 153).

Tailor's chalk Use this sewing notion to mark stitching lines or to outline a pattern shape on fabric.

Tracing paper Before you begin sewing, we recommend getting some tracing paper, such as Swedish Tracing Paper, which is stronger and more flexible than tissue paper, to trace the template patterns in this book.

tip: *All fabric widths for the projects, unless otherwise noted, are 44"–45". To make sure you will have enough fabric, we calculated yardage assuming that usable fabric is 40" wide.*

CHRISTMAS WONDERLAND

It is only fitting to begin with Christmas because, for us, Christmas is the holiday that gave birth to all the others. Our childhood Noels taught us the importance of gathering together with family and friends to feast and remember. We love Christmas because it is a time of magical transformation. The house becomes a winter wonderland; the living room, a depot for arriving presents.

As children, we learned from our parents that handmade touches are important and that it is more fun if you are allowed to hold the decorations. We use the same rules of playfulness in our own homes. When we invite everyone to Christmas dinner, we allow our imaginations to take over.

The table is rich with different textures—the softness of the velvet and felt, the smoothness of the china, the scratchiness of the miniature trees. Rings of felt holly leaves and berries adorn the napkins. The final touch is the most charming of all Christmas desserts—the Yule log. Our version is decadently chocolate and dusted with snow.

Holly Berry Napkin Rings

As Christmas draws closer, we look for opportunities to sit and sew in a cozy spot by the fire or in front of a favorite holiday film. This project fits the bill. After the cutting and decorative machine sewing are complete, the leaves and berries come together with ease.

FINISHED SIZE:
Napkin ring 1 3/8"
(inside diameter);
berries 1/2" across

Materials and Supplies

Makes 1 napkin ring.

- Light green felt: 8″ × 10″
- Medium green felt: 8″ × 8″
- Dark green felt: 8″ × 8″
- Dark red felt: 4″ × 4″
- Cardboard tube: empty wrapping paper roll or other cardboard tube such as a paper towel roll
- Polyfill stuffing or batting: small handful
- Freezer paper

Cutting

The template patterns are on pullout page P1.

Light green felt:

Cut 3 leaves using the leaf template pattern.

Cut 1 piece 1″ × 5⅞″ for the outer napkin ring.

Cut 1 piece 1″ × 5¼″ for the inner napkin ring.

Medium green felt:

Cut 4 leaves using the leaf template pattern.

Dark green felt:

Cut 3 leaves using the leaf template pattern.

Dark red felt:

Cut 3 circles using the berry template pattern.

Cardboard tube:

Cut a ¾″-wide band from the cardboard tube.

tip: *The base of a medium-sized spool of thread makes a perfect circle template pattern for the berries.*

INSTRUCTIONS

Refer to Sewing Felt (page 155).

1. Decorate the leaves by machine stitching down the center of each leaf.

2. Insert the short piece of light green felt inside the cardboard tube. Wrap the wider piece around the outside of the tube. Whipstitch (page 154) around each edge.

3. To make the berries, baste around the edge of a red circle and pull the thread to gather. Before you cinch the circle completely closed, insert stuffing into the circle to create a ball shape. Sew the opening closed securely. Repeat with the other 2 circles.

4. Lay a leaf at an angle on the napkin ring and whipstitch around the bottom, curved edge of the leaf to attach. Arrange the next leaf on top and sew, creating an alcove where the berries will sit.

5. Continue arranging leaves, alternating colors, until you have a pleasing arrangement that wraps all the way around the napkin ring.

6. Sew the berries in place by hand.

Santa's Sleigh Centerpiece

Santa's sleigh is small, so we splurged on a rich velvet, which looks beautiful against the silver lamé trim and red sateen lining. We'll show you how to make your own piping trim out of any fabric. Santa's faithful reindeer are sewn from felt and stand up thanks to some cleverly placed cotton swabs.

FINISHED SIZE:
Sleigh 6½″ wide × 4″ tall;
reindeer 5″ tall

Sleigh

Materials and Supplies

- Red velvet or velveteen: ¼ yard for sled exterior

- Red sateen: ¼ yard for lining

- Silver lamé: ¼ yard for piping

- Cotton piping: ¼″ wide, 1⅓ yards

- Zipper foot for sewing machine

- Interfacing:
  ½ yard heavy-duty interfacing (20″ wide), such as Pellon Peltex 70 Ultra-Firm Stabilizer

  ½ yard lightweight fusible interfacing (20″ wide), such as Pellon 911FF Fusible Featherweight

Cutting

The template patterns are on pullout page P1. The sleigh template patterns should be enlarged 200%. The reindeer template patterns do not require enlargement.

Red velvet:

Cut 2 (1 and 1 reversed) sleigh pieces and 1 gusset using the template patterns.

Red sateen:

Cut 2 (1 and 1 reversed) sleigh pieces and 1 gusset using the template patterns.

Silver lamé:

Cut 4 bias strips 2″ × 12½″.

Heavy-duty interfacing:

Cut 2 (1 and 1 reversed) sleigh pieces and 1 gusset, using the dashed markings for interfacing on the template patterns.

Lightweight fusible interfacing:

Cut 2 (1 and 1 reversed) sleigh pieces and 1 gusset using the outside lines on the template patterns.

INSTRUCTIONS

1. Center the heavy-duty interfacing on the wrong side of a red velvet sleigh piece. Layer the lightweight fusible interfacing on top. Follow the manufacturer's directions to fuse the interfacings in place. Repeat with remaining interfacing and velvet sleigh and gusset pieces.

2. Sew 2 lamé bias strips together end to end. Fold the bias strip in half lengthwise with wrong sides together. Press lightly using low heat, first testing a scrap piece of fabric to ensure the iron will not melt the lamé. Repeat with remaining lamé bias strips.

3. Open the folded lamé strip and place the cotton piping along the crease. Close the lamé around the piping and, using your sewing machine's zipper foot, sew as close to the cotton piping as possible. Trim seam to ¼″. Repeat for the remaining strip.

4. Sew an exterior sleigh piece to the exterior gusset, beginning at the back of the sleigh and sewing along the bottom to the front. Some of the gusset will extend beyond the front of the sleigh. Repeat for the opposite side. Trim seams, cut corners, and turn right side out. Press.

5. Repeat Step 4 for the lining pieces, leaving a 3″ gap along the bottom of a side of the sleigh. Clip curves and corners.

6. Starting at the back, pin lamé piping trim around the upper edge of the outer sleigh. Pin all the way around the side edges and up the loose flap at the front. Baste piping in place. Trim any excess piping. Repeat for the other half of the sleigh, overlapping the piping at the back.

7. Insert the exterior sleigh (right side out) into the sleigh lining (wrong side out) with right sides facing each other. Stitch around the top circumference of the sleigh. Trim seams and turn the piece through the gap left in the lining. Slipstitch the opening in the lining closed. Push the lining into the sleigh. Using a tailor's ham or a folded towel inserted inside the sleigh, lightly press.

8. Roll the front flap around a pencil to create a curved railing for the front of the sleigh. Hand stitch in place.

Reindeer

Materials and Supplies

Makes 1 reindeer.

- Tan felt: 8½" × 11"
- Brown felt: 4" × 4"
- White felt: 4" × 4"
- Crimson felt: 2" × 7"
- Embroidery thread: dark brown (and red if you want your reindeer to be Rudolph)
- Silver cord: ¾ yard for harness
- Card stock: 5" × 5" scrap (a cereal box works well)
- Cotton swabs: 3
- Polyfill stuffing or batting: small handful

Cutting

The template patterns are on pullout page P1.

Tan felt:
Cut 2 (1 and 1 reversed) reindeer body pieces.

Brown felt:
Cut 2 (1 and 1 reversed) antler pieces.

White felt:
Cut 1 chest piece.

Crimson felt:
Cut 1 strip ¼" × 4" for the harness.
Cut 2 strips ⅜" × 6" for the harness.

Silver cord:
Cut 2 pieces 12" long.

Card stock:
Cut 1 reindeer body, using dotted lines on template pattern.

INSTRUCTIONS

Refer to Sewing Felt (page 155) to sew the reindeer pieces and to Hand Stitches (page 154) for embroidery stitch instructions.

1. Sew the white chest piece to the front of a reindeer body.

2. Embroider the face on the reindeer using 2 strands of brown embroidery floss. Use a satin stitch for the nose and a French knot for the eye.

3. With wrong sides together, sandwich 2 reindeer pieces around the card stock body and whipstitch around the outside edge of the body, leaving openings at the base of each foot, the back, and the top of the head. Using a chopstick, gently insert stuffing in the back of the reindeer.

4. Stitch the back closed, leaving the head open to insert the antlers in the next step.

5. Sew 2 antler pieces together using a whipstitch and insert through the head opening, over the card stock base. Stitch in place.

6. Cut an end off each of the 3 cotton swabs, and insert each cut end into a leg.

7. Using the project photo (page 14) as a guide, wrap a ⅜" × 6" strip of crimson felt around the reindeer, coming over the back and across the chest. Trim if necessary and secure with hot glue or stitch in place. Wrap the other ⅜" × 6" strip over the back and between the front 2 legs, and secure. Wrap the ¼" × 4" strip of felt around the reindeer's back and stomach, and secure. Place an end of a silver cord underneath the wider strip of felt and secure. Repeat on other side.

Rooftop Place Cards

These felt houses are inspired by the Christmas villages we have always admired in store windows and other people's homes. We embroidered our guests' names on top in white so it looked like the letters were written in snow.

FINISHED SIZE:
3" wide × 4" tall

Materials and Supplies

Makes 1 house.

- **Tan felt:** ⅛ yard

- **Brown felt:** ⅛ yard

- **White felt:** ⅛ yard

- **Card stock:** 8″ × 8″ piece
  (We used an old cereal box.)

- **Embroidery floss:** green, red, and white

- **Tissue paper**

- **Polyfill stuffing or batting**

Cutting

The template patterns are on pullout page P1.

Tan felt:

Cut 2 house pieces using the template pattern.

Cut 2 pieces 3″ × 4⅜″ for the sides.

Cut 1 piece 3″ × 3″ for the bottom.

Brown felt:

Cut 1 door using the template pattern.

Cut 2 pieces 2¼″ × 3″ for the roof.

Cut 12 squares ⅜″ × ⅜″ for the
windowpanes. (It is easiest to cut
a strip ⅜″ × 5″ and then cut the
strip into ⅜″ × ⅜″ squares.)*

White felt:

Cut 2 large snowdrifts for the roof
using the template pattern.

Cut 3 small snowdrifts for the windows
using the template pattern.*

Card stock:

Cut 2 house pieces using the template pattern.

* See Tip, page 19.

Handmade Hostess

INSTRUCTIONS

Refer to Sewing Felt (page 155) and Hand Stitches (page 154) to assemble and decorate the house.

Decorating the House

1. Decorate a side of the house using the photo (page 18) as a guide. Sew on the window-panes for the 2 side windows and then the small snowdrifts under each window.

2. Sew the door and upper window to the front of the house. Sew a small white snowdrift under the front window.

3. Using 2 strands of green embroidery floss, stitch a small wreath on the front door using a chain stitch. Embellish with 3 French knots using 2 strands of red embroidery floss.

4. Write the guest's name on tissue paper and place it over a brown roof piece. Embroider the guest's name on the rooftop using a back-stitch with 2 strands of white embroidery floss. Stitch through both the tissue paper and the felt. When you are finished, tear away the tissue paper.

tip: *We decorated only the front and a side of the house. If you prefer to have windows on both sides, cut 8 additional windowpanes and 2 additional small snowdrifts.*

Assembling the House

1. With wrong sides together, use a blanket stitch to attach the side of the house to the front piece, starting at the top (the peak of the roof) and working your way down to the bottom. Repeat for the other side of the house.

2. Using a blanket stitch, sew the side pieces together along the top edge.

3. Use a blanket stitch to attach the back of the house between the 2 side pieces.

4. Slide the card stock house pieces into the sewn house shape. Stuff the house with polyfill or batting.

5. Attach the base of the house using a blanket stitch, stopping to adjust the stuffing before the bottom is completely attached. Finish stitching the base closed.

6. Whipstitch the dark brown roof pieces together along the top edges. Place the dark brown roof over the tan house shape, making sure that the guest's name appears over the windows on the decorated side. Blanket stitch the roof to the house along the angled roofline on the front and back.

7. Use a blanket stitch to attach the large white roof snowdrifts together along the top edge. Place the snowdrifts on top of the house and whipstitch into place all the way around the edge of each snowdrift.

Simple Yule Log

A traditional recipe can be a highlight of this holiday, and for my family, the Yule log is just that. It doesn't hurt that it is also one of the most beautiful and tasty Christmas desserts. Presenting it at the end of the meal with a fresh dusting of powdered-sugar snow feels like a celebration in and of itself.

INGREDIENTS

5 large eggs, separated

⅔ cup sugar

2 tablespoons all-purpose flour

3 tablespoons unsweetened cocoa powder

Vanilla Filling (recipe follows):

    2 packages (3.5 oz. each) instant vanilla pudding

    2 cups heavy cream

    1 cup milk

    2 teaspoons vanilla extract

Chocolate Buttercream Icing (see page 59)

Nonstick cooking spray

Powdered sugar

DIRECTIONS

You will need a 10˝ × 15˝ baking sheet with a 1˝ lip; and waxed, freezer, or parchment paper.

Prepare the Vanilla Filling (below right) and refrigerate.

To make Chocolate Buttercream Icing, use the recipe for Buttercream Icing in Petit Fours (page 59). Omit 1 teaspoon of vanilla extract and add in ¼ cup of cocoa powder. You may need to add a couple of extra table-spoons of milk to make it soft and spreadable.

In a large bowl, beat the egg yolks with an electric mixer until light-colored and fluffy. Mix in the sugar, flour, and cocoa powder. In a separate bowl, whip the egg whites until soft to medium peaks form. Fold the mixtures together gently until they are thoroughly combined.

Line the baking sheet with the paper. Push the paper in at the edges so that the batter does not run out; spray with nonstick cooking spray. Evenly spread the batter into the prepared baking sheet.

Bake at 350°F for approximately 17 minutes. The cake is done when you touch it and it springs back. Do not overbake. Let the cake cool on the paper before filling. Cut away any hard (overbaked) edges with a sharp knife.

Gently lift the paper and remove paper and cake from the pan. Lay it on a counter. Evenly spread the filling on the cake.

Now you are ready to roll the cake into a log shape, starting at one end and using the paper to help the cake keep its shape. As the cake comes down on the first roll and begins to curl under itself, gently pull back the paper so it does not get rolled into the cake. After the whole cake is rolled in this manner, apply a layer of Chocolate Buttercream Icing to the outside of the cake and let it chill 30–60 minutes until the frosting is firm. To achieve the bark look, gently drag a fork over the log from one end to the other. Lightly sprinkle with powdered sugar.

VANILLA FILLING Using an electric mixer with a whisk attachment at high speed, combine the **instant vanilla pudding, heavy cream, milk,** and **vanilla extract.** Beat until fluffy.

To: My Sweetheart
2 Lovers Lane
Cupid's Corner, XO

HANDLE WITH CARE

SPECIAL DELIVERY VALENTINE EXPRESS MAIL

VALENTINE'S DAY CELEBRATION

For Valentine's Day, we wanted to honor the very heartbeat of the holiday—and in our opinion, it's all about the mail. To celebrate, we created a messenger bag just the right size for carting off stacks of valentines to school. Our valentine table is festive, with specially decorated sugar cookies, embroidered love note napkins, and a playful but pretty floral arrangement.

Whether or not you have a special someone in your life, we hope the ideas here get you excited about the day. Leave a valentine in someone else's mailbox—it can be almost as much fun as finding something sweet in your own.

Love Note Napkins

To: My Sweetheart
2 Lovers Lane
Cupid's Corner, XO

These love notes are more permanent than the paper kind, so we recommend settling into a comfy spot and putting some love into every stitch. Fold the completed napkin into an envelope shape and slip a handwritten note inside. This is a beginner-friendly embroidery project; the back of your work will not show.

FINISHED SIZE:
17" × 17"

Materials and Supplies

Makes 1 napkin.

- **White cotton fabric:** 5/8 yard
- **White wool felt:** 2″ × 2″
- **Embroidery floss:** red
- **Pen:** brown fine-point transfer pen (We used a Pigma Micron 005.*)
- **Masking tape**
- **Inkjet printer fabric:** for stamp (see Resources, page 158)
- **Computer scanner and inkjet printer:** for stamp

* This pen is permanent but very thin, so it will not be visible once you have stitched over the pattern.

INSTRUCTIONS

The stamp image and template pattern are on page 27.

Embroidering the Napkin

I. Cut 2 squares of white cotton 17½″ × 17½″.

2. For the embroidered "address," transfer the pattern using the text placement illustration (page 26) for guidance. Tape the pattern to a sunny window. Lay the fabric over the pattern and tape it in place. Trace the pattern carefully using the pen.

3. Backstitch the letters using 2 strands of red embroidery floss, referring to Hand Stitches (page 154).

To: My Sweetheart
2 Lovers Lane
Cupid's Corner, XO

Text placement

FROM: Your Valentine

tip: *Want to make the napkins even more personal? Consider using your guests' names and addresses instead of the one we used. Simply write out the letters using your best handwriting (or print them from a computer using a plain font) and transfer to the fabric.*

Creating the Stamp

I. Use a flatbed scanner to scan the stamp image (below). Print it on the inkjet printer fabric, and follow the manufacturer's instructions to heat set the ink.

2. Cut a stamp out of felt using the template pattern (below), referring to Sewing Felt (page 155) for the cutting technique.

Printed fabric stamp image   Stamp felt template

3. Layer the printed stamp on top of the felt and stitch it to the napkin, sewing around all 4 sides and leaving the edges raw.

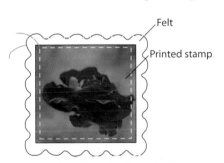

Felt

Printed stamp

Stitch stamp to napkin through all layers.

tip: *You could also make your own stamp using leftover pieces of fabric or felt. There is no wrong way to do this. Experiment and have fun!*

Sewing the Napkin

I. With right sides together and using a ¼" seam allowance, sew the 2 squares 17½" × 17½" around all 4 sides, leaving a 3" opening on one side.

2. Clip corners, turn the napkin right side out, and press.

3. Hand stitch the opening closed using a slip stitch, or topstitch ⅛" from the edge around all 4 sides.

Fold napkin to create envelope.

Special Delivery Centerpiece

This simple cardboard box makes for a surprisingly elegant floral arrangement. If floral arranging is not your thing, you can bring your own cube vase to a professional florist and have that part done for you. All you will need to do is slip the vase into the box and deliver!

FINISHED BOX SIZE: 6¼" cube

Materials and Supplies

- **White label paper:** 8½" × 11"

- **Scrapbook paper:**
  2 sheets, 12" × 12"

- **Cardboard box:** 6" cube*

- **Clear tape**

- **Waterproof tape:** Do not use stem tape, since it has no adhesive. You can substitute masking tape, but be careful not to get it wet.

- **Roses and carnations:** We used 9 large roses, 12 miniature roses, and 12 carnations.

- **Ribbon:** ½" wide, 40" length

* If you have a vase of a different size, find or create a box that is just slightly larger than the vase.

On the label in the photo:

HANDLE WITH CARE

SPECIAL DELIVERY VALENTINE EXPRESS MAIL

To: My Sweetheart
2 Lovers Lane
Cupid's Corner, XO

INSTRUCTIONS

Decorating the Box

1. Scan or photocopy the label template pattern (at right) and print it onto white label paper.

2. Cut out strips of scrapbook paper 6" × 12" and tape them to the box, overlapping on the sides to hide the seams.

3. Personalize the mailing label and attach.

4. Fold the flaps of the box inside or leave them out and decorate them with paper.

5. Tie the ribbon around the top edge of the box as shown in the project photo (page 28). Trim ends.

tip: *The wider the opening on the vase, the more flowers you will need to fill it. To keep costs down, consider using a smaller cube. You could also use more fillers, such as carnations or daisies, in place of roses.*

HANDLE WITH CARE

SPECIAL DELIVERY: VALENTINE EXPRESS MAIL

Label template pattern

Arranging the Flowers

1. Fill the vase half full of water and create a 3 × 3 grid using waterproof tape. Beginning with the carnations, take a flower, remove any excess leaves and greenery, and trim the stem to the desired length. Arrange in the grid.

2. Repeat this process with the roses. The goal is a dense arrangement of flowers all the same height with no tape showing. Slide the vase into the box.

29

Valentine's Day Celebration

Mail Carrier Messenger Bag

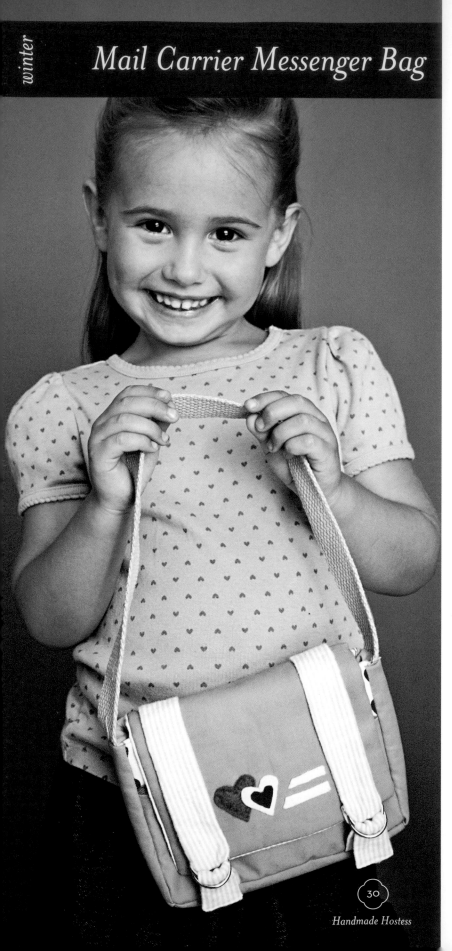

The mail carrier messenger bag is sized just right for petite valentine envelopes. We sewed this one in pink, but with a few changes in materials, you could make a boy-friendly version as well. This bag was so popular with the kids, we had a hard time keeping it on the table long enough for photographs.

FINISHED SIZE: Approximately 6″ wide × 4½″ tall × 1½″ deep

Materials and Supplies

- Pink fabric: ¼ yard for exterior

- Pink-and-white striped fabric: ¼ yard for flap lining and buckle straps

- Heart print fabric: scrap at least 5″ × 6½″ for front

- Floral print fabric: ¼ yard for lining

- Pale pink solid fabric: ¼ yard for lining

- Interfacing: ¼ yard lightweight interfacing (20″ wide), such as Pellon 911FF Fusible Featherweight

- Scraps of felt: pink, white, and red for emblem

- D-rings: ¾″ wide, set of 4

- Pink cotton webbing: 1″ wide × 18½″ long

- Pink rickrack: ⅝″ wide, 6½″ piece

Cutting

The emblem template patterns are on pullout page P1.

Pink fabric:

Cut 1 piece 5″ × 6½″ for the back.

Cut 1 piece 3½″ × 6½″ for the pocket.

Cut 2 pieces 2″ × 5″ for the sides.

Cut 1 piece 2″ × 6½″ for the bottom.

Cut 1 piece 5½″ × 6¼″ for the flap.

Pink-and-white stripe:

Cut 1 piece 5½″ × 6¼″ for the flap lining.

Cut 2 strips 2½″ × 3¼″ and 2 strips 2½″ × 6¼″ for the buckle straps.

Heart print:

Cut 1 piece 5″ × 6½″ for the front.

Floral print:

Cut 2 pieces 5″ × 6½″ for the lining front and back.

Cut 1 piece 3½″ × 6½″ for the pocket lining.

Pale pink solid:

Cut 2 pieces 2″ × 5″ for the lining sides.

Cut 1 piece 2″ × 6½″ for the lining bottom.

Fusible interfacing:

Cut 2 pieces 4½″ × 6″ for the front and back.

Cut 2 pieces 1½″ × 4½″ for the sides.

Cut 1 piece 1½″ × 6″ for the bottom.

Cut 1 piece 5″ × 5¾″ for the flap.

Cut 1 piece 3″ × 6″ for the pocket.

INSTRUCTIONS

Use a ¼″ seam allowance unless otherwise noted. See the illustrations in Hand Stitches (page 154).

Making the Buckle Straps

1. Fold a 2½″ × 3¼″ strip in half lengthwise with right sides together, and sew along the length of the strip and across a short side. Clip corners, turn, and press. Repeat with the other 2½″ × 3¼″ strip.

2. Fold a 2½″ × 6¼″ strip in half lengthwise with right sides together, and sew the longest edge. Turn strip right side out and press. Fold the strip around 2 of the D-rings, tucking the raw edge under, and hand stitch in place using a blind hem stitch (page 154). Repeat with the other 2½″ × 6¼″ strip.

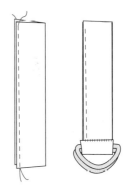

Making the Bag Body

1. Follow the manufacturer's instructions to fuse the interfacing pieces to the center of the wrong sides of the pink back and heart print front pieces, the sides, the bottom, the pocket, and the flap.

2. Refer to Sewing Felt (page 155) to cut out the pink, red, and white emblems from felt.

3. Arrange the felt emblem pieces on the flap, referring to the photo (page 30) for placement. Center the emblem pieces approximately 1¼″ from the bottom edge of the fabric. Hand stitch in place using a whipstitch (page 154) and matching embroidery floss.

4. Pin the rickrack to the pocket front, lining up the top of the rickrack with the top of the fabric. Lay the pocket lining on top, right sides together, and stitch the top edge of the pocket using a ¼" seam allowance (Figure 1). Turn and press.

5. Baste the pocket to the front panel with the pocket lining facing the right side of the front panel. Stitch along the bottom and sides of the pocket using a ⅛" seam allowance and a long stitch length (Figure 2). This unit is now referred to as the front.

6. With right sides together, sandwich the 2 short straps (from Making the Buckle Straps, Step 1) between the front and the exterior bottom piece. Place the straps so the outside edges are approximately ⅞" from each side edge. Sew along the bottom, starting and stopping ¼" from the sides (Figure 3).

7. With right sides together and using a ¼" seam allowance, sew the side gussets to either side of the front, starting at the top and ending ¼" from the bottom (Figure 4).

8. With right sides together, sew each side to the bottom, starting and stopping ¼" from the side (Figure 5).

9. With right sides together, sew the back exterior fabric to the bottom, starting and stopping ¼" from each side. Sew the back to the sides (Figure 6). Turn the bag right side out.

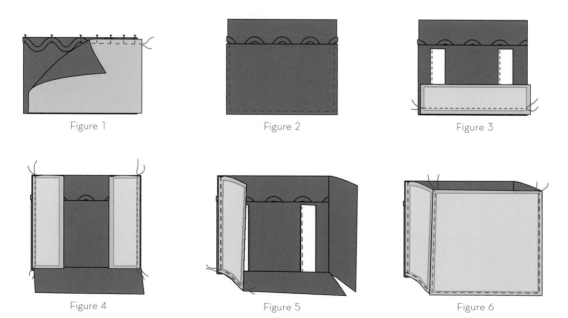

Figure 1   Figure 2   Figure 3

Figure 4   Figure 5   Figure 6

Handmade Hostess

IO. Place an end of the pink cotton webbing on the top edge of a side, aligning the raw edges. Refer to Figure 7 for guidance. Baste using a 1/8" seam allowance. Repeat to attach the other end of the webbing to the remaining side.

II. With right sides together, sew the front flap to the flap lining along the side and bottom edges. Clip corners, turn, and press.

I2. Pin the flap to the top edge of the bag back, sandwiching the long straps (from Making the Buckle Straps, Step 2) between the layers. The outer edge of each strap should be approximately 3/4" from either side of the front flap. Check to make sure that the upper straps will line up properly with the lower straps when the bag is closed. Baste using a 1/8" seam allowance (Figure 7).

I3. With right sides together, sew a front lining piece to the bottom lining, leaving a 3" opening in the center of the seam.

I4. With right sides together, continue to assemble the bag's lining as you did with the exterior in Steps 7–9.

I5. Insert the exterior bag, right side facing out, into the bag lining, wrong side facing out (Figure 8). Pin around the top, making sure the straps are not twisted or caught in the seam. Stitch around the top of the bag using a 1/4" seam allowance. Turn the bag right side out through the opening in the lining and hand stitch the gap in the lining closed. Push the lining inside the exterior bag and press.

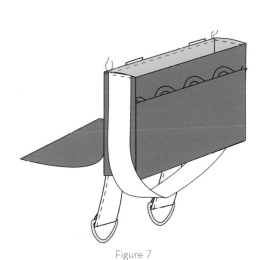

Figure 7

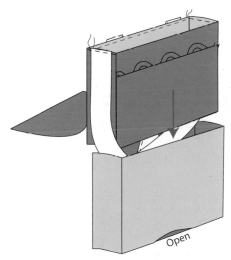

Open

Figure 8

Valentine Sugar Cookies

Cookies are one of those treats that take me right back to my child-hood, when I would come home from school to find a plate of sugar cookies waiting on the kitchen table. For these, try writing out a sweet message in icing to give to a beloved—or you could just make them for yourself as a sweet treat!

INGREDIENTS

Makes 3–5 dozen cookies.

1 cup butter (2 sticks) softened

1 cup sugar

2 large eggs

2½ teaspoons vanilla extract

½ teaspoon salt

3 cups flour

1 teaspoon baking soda

Royal Icing (recipe follows):

    4 cups powdered sugar

    3 tablespoons meringue powder (avail-able at your local craft or baking store)

    Gel food coloring

DIRECTIONS

You will need a baking sheet that fits in your refrigerator, parchment paper or a nonstick mat, rolling pin, cookie cutters, and a piping bag. If you don't have a piping bag, use a thick plastic food storage bag with the bottom corner snipped to the size you need.

Prepare the Royal Icing and set aside.

Using a mixer, combine the butter and sugar. Add the eggs, vanilla extract, and salt. In a separate bowl, whisk the flour and baking soda together by hand until well mixed. Stir the flour mixture into the egg and butter mixture.

Place the dough in an airtight container in the refrigerator and allow it to chill until hard. On a heavily floured surface, roll out the chilled dough to about ¼˝ thick. To keep it from sticking, lift it often and reflour the work surface and rolling pin. Use a cookie cutter dusted with flour to cut out shapes.

Place the cookies on a baking sheet lined with parchment paper. Chill for 20 minutes.

Bake in a preheated 350°F oven for approximately 10 minutes, until the edges are golden brown. Let the cookies cool a little on the baking sheet, and then carefully transfer them to a wire rack to cool completely.

Dunk the tops of the cookies into the runny Royal Icing to apply a thin coat. Decorate the cookies using a piping bag with a small piping attachment. A #2 or #3 piping tip works best. Add some dashes along the edge of each cookie to mimic stitches, which look so cute!

Store the cookies in an airtight container for up to a week.

ROYAL ICING   With a whisk attachment on your mixer, combine the **powdered sugar,** the **meringue powder,** and ½–¾ cup **warm water.** (Add the full ¾ cup for a runny icing consistency.) Whip until the mixture turns white and glossy, and forms peaks or ribbons (2–4 minutes). Color with **gel food coloring.**

Note: You can use liquid food coloring, but add it before you finish adding all of the water so the icing doesn't get *too* runny.

Find your lucky clover.

TREATS

Find your lucky clover.

ST. PATRICK'S DAY PARTY

When we were children, our imaginations needed hardly any encouragement at all. We saw elves, leprechauns, and secret doors everywhere we went. St. Patrick's Day was permission to do what we did best—look for evidence of secret things. Now, as adults, we love to keep the game going.

For this backyard party, we playfully incorporated a few formal details, such as table assignments, to create an environment that made both the adults and the children feel special. A festive tablecloth serves as the backdrop for a drink station, place card holders, and truffles. Pint-sized wooden drawers stuffed with moss and gold coins show off the leprechaun hat place cards and tie in with our magical garland—a miniature laundry line of leprechaun clothes.

We covered the main tables in simple white tablecloths and wrapped them with ribbons. Green flocking powder and a collection of small wooden letters became cheeky signs—"Kiss Me, I'm Irish," and "Luck."

If you have young children around, there are lots of ways to get them involved in the planning. They may even let you borrow some of their dollhouse-sized furniture to use as part of the décor.

Leprechaun Clothes Banner

There are a few tricks to hand sewing a wardrobe of leprechaun clothes. However, even with the shortcuts we'll show you, this is a project best started early. In our opinion, the results are absolutely worth it. After the party is over, the banner would make a wonderful decoration for a child's room.

FINISHED SIZE:
Approximately
3½" tall × 45" long

Materials and Supplies

- **White cotton:** ¼ yard for shirt

- **Green damask print:** 2" × 4" scrap for bow tie

- **Green crushed velvet:** ¼ yard for jacket

- **Green floral print fabric:** ⅛ yard for boxer shorts

- **Green striped fabric:** 4" × 12" scrap for stockings

- **Green polka dot fabric:** ⅛ yard for pants

- **Green satin or silky fabric:** 1" × 1" scrap for jacket pocket square

- **Buttons:** 3 clear ⅛" shirt buttons for shirt; 2 clear ⅛" buttons for jacket

materials and supplies continued

- **Thin elastic ponytail holders:**
  2 for waistbands of pants
  and boxer shorts (*alternative:*
  12″ piece of narrow elastic)

- **Wooden clothespins:** 10
  miniature (1″) clothespins

- **Nylon cord:** 1½ yards for
  the clothesline (We used
  Darice Metallic Jewelry
  Cord in white/gold.)

Cutting

*The template patterns are on
pullout page P1.*

White cotton fabric:

Cut 2 (1 and 1 reversed)
shirt fronts.

Cut 1 shirt back on fold.

Cut 2 cuffs.

Cut 1 collar.

Green damask fabric:

Cut 2 bows.

Cut 1 tie.

Green crushed velvet fabric:

Cut 2 (1 and 1 reversed)
jacket facings.

Cut 2 (1 and 1 reversed)
jacket fronts.

Cut 1 jacket back on fold.

Cut 1 jacket pocket.

Green floral fabric:

Cut 2 boxer shorts.

Green striped fabric:

Cut 4 (2 and 2 reversed)
stockings.

Green polka dot fabric:

Cut 2 pants.

INSTRUCTIONS

All seams for the leprechaun shirt, jacket, and stockings are
backstitched (page 154) by hand using a hand-sewing needle
and coordinating thread.

tip: *When hand sewing small items such as stuffed toys
and doll clothes, it can be helpful to use a piece of tissue
paper as a guide. Trace the pattern onto the tissue paper,
including stitching lines, and lay the tissue paper over the
fabric as you sew. Stitch through both the fabric and the
tissue paper at the same time. When done, tear off the tissue
paper and discard.*

Shirt

1. To hem the shirt back, fold the fabric under ⅛″ and press.
Turn the fabric under ⅛″ again and sew the hem.

2. On the shirt front, fold the front facing in
toward the sleeve with right sides together,
aligning the fabric along the side seam.
Lay the tissue-paper template pattern on
top of the fabric, and stitch the hem and
neck, following the stitching guides on the
tissue paper (Figure 1). Trim excess fabric,
clip curves, turn, and press. Repeat for the
other side.

Figure 1

3. With right sides together, stitch the front to the back along the sleeve, side seam, and top using the tissue-paper template pattern as a guide (Figure 2). The fabric will not match up perfectly. Clip curves, turn, and press. Repeat for the other side.

Figure 2

4. Prepare the collar by folding fabric in half lengthwise with right sides together. Then fold up each long raw edge ⅛" to create a W shape (Figure 3). Stitch the short sides using a ¼" seam allowance. Clip corners and turn the piece right side out. Pin the collar to the neck opening and whipstitch (page 154) in place. Fold collar to the outside and press.

Figure 3

5. To create cuffs, fold fabric in half lengthwise with right sides together. Then fold up each long raw edge ⅛" to create a W shape. Sew the side edges using a ¼" seam allowance. Turn fabric right side out, and stitch to sleeve opening (Figure 4). Cuffs will be wider than the sleeves so they look like French cuffs.

Figure 4

6. To create the tie for the center of the bow tie, first fold the tie in half lengthwise with right sides together. Fold up each long edge ⅛" to create a W shape. Stitch as close to the edge as possible along the sides. Turn right side out and press. Place the bow pieces right sides together, and stitch around the bottom and side edges using a ⅛" seam allowance (Figure 5). Turn right side out, fold in the raw edges, and topstitch along the folds. Wrap the tie around the center of the bow, and hand stitch in place. Attach to the shirt and add 3 buttons.

Figure 5

Jacket

1. Hem the jacket back as in Step 1 for the shirt (page 39).

2. Lay the facing on top of the jacket front with right sides of the fabric both facing up. The facing of the jacket will be the wrong side of the velvet to create contrast. Stitch along the neck, front, and bottom edges to attach facing (Figure 6). Do not stitch the side seam underneath the arm. Trim excess fabric, clip curves, turn, and press. Repeat with remaining jacket front and facing.

Figure 6

3. Attach the pocket on 1 jacket front piece using a slipstitch, turning under the fabric by ⅛" as you stitch.

Handmade Hostess

4. With right sides together, sew a front piece to the back along the underarm, side seams, and shoulder. Repeat to attach the other front piece.

5. Turn the fabric under ¼" along the sleeve opening and stitch in place (Figure 7).

Figure 7

6. Fold under the neck opening at the back and stitch.

7. Fold back the lapels along each front and press. Stitch the front of the jacket closed. Attach 2 buttons.

8. Fold the 1" × 1" square of silky fabric and slip inside the pocket as a pocket square.

Pants and Boxer Shorts

1. To hem the bottom edge of the pant legs, fold fabric under ⅛" and finger press. Turn again and stitch. The first 2 steps can be sewn by machine if preferred.

2. Fold a pant piece in half with right sides together, and stitch the inseams using a ¼" seam allowance (Figure 8). Trim seams to ⅛". Repeat for the other leg.

3. Turn a leg right side out and insert into the other leg with right sides together. Match up curves, and hand stitch the crotch seam using a ¼" seam allowance (Figure 9). Turn pants right side out.

4. Fold the top edge of fabric around the ponytail elastic to create a casing, and stitch by hand. Try using the miniature wooden clothespins to hold the elastic in place while you stitch (Figure 10).

5. Repeat Steps 1–4 with the boxer shorts pieces to make the boxer shorts.

Figure 8   Figure 9

Figure 10

Stockings

1. To hem the top edge of the stockings, fold under ⅛" and finger press. Turn again and stitch. Repeat for all 4 stocking pieces.

2. Align 2 stocking pieces with right sides together. Backstitch around the dotted line using the tissue-paper template pattern as a guide. Clip curves and trim seams, being careful not to cut through the stitching. Turn right side out and press. Repeat with the remaining 2 stocking pieces.

tip: *When turning small pieces, such as the stockings, be patient. If the seam begins to come undone, try to salvage your work by tucking the stray threads back inside the seam with a needle and applying a fray stop product such as Dritz Fray Check.*

Leprechaun Hat Place Card Holders

Ed Park

The leprechaun hats are best worked in batches as an assembly-
line project. Most of the work is in cutting out the pieces and
preparing the supplies. Once you get going, the hats come
together quickly with just three hand-sewn seams.

The leprechaun hats are best worked in batches as an assembly-
line project. Most of the work is in cutting out the pieces and
preparing the supplies. Once you get going, the hats come
together quickly with just three hand-sewn seams.

FINISHED SIZE:
3″ wide × 2″ tall

Materials and Supplies

Makes 1 place card holder.

- **Green felt:** 8″ × 9″

- **Thin cardboard:** 3″ × 7″
  piece for hat side (We used
  a leftover cereal box.)

- **Embroidery floss:** green

- **Stiff cardboard:** such as
  mat board, for buckle

- **Ribbon:** ³⁄₈″ wide, 7″ piece

- **Heavy card stock:**
  ⁵⁄₈″ × 2¼″ strip
  for place card

- **Shamrock stickers:** 2 (or
  gold label paper and a
  heart-shaped hole punch)

- **Brass head pin:** 3″ gold
  plated (found in jewelry
  section of craft store)

- **Glue and gold glitter**

- **Craft knife**

- **Hot glue gun**

INSTRUCTIONS

Creating the Hat

The template patterns are on pullout page P1.

I. For each hat, cut a top, a brim, and 2 side pieces from green felt. Refer to Sewing Felt (page 155) for cutting technique. Cut a side piece from thin cardboard along the dotted lines on the template pattern.

2. Form a felt side piece into a tube shape with the ends just slightly overlapping. The tube will be wider at the top than at the bottom. Check the diameter of the top and bottom against the top and brim felt pieces, and adjust the diameter as necessary. Whipstitch along the side seam. Form the thin cardboard side piece into a tube, and insert it into the felt tube. The ends of the cardboard will overlap. Repeat with the remaining piece of felt so that the cardboard is completely concealed in felt (Figure 1).

3. Place the top piece on the hat, and whipstitch around the edge (Figure 2).

4. Turn the hat upside down and lay the brim piece over the bottom opening. Whipstitch the inner brim to the hat base (Figure 3).

5. Cut the buckle out of thin mat board using a craft knife.

6. Using a paintbrush, coat the buckle with glue and sprinkle with glitter. Let dry.

7. Cut ribbon into 2 strips 3½" long. Fold the strips around either side of the buckle, and hot glue in place (Figure 4). Place the buckle on the hat and glue the ends of the ribbon securely.

8. Write a guest's name on a ⅝" × 2¼" piece of card stock.

9. Attach the place card to a pin with a dot of hot glue, and cover with 2 shamrock stickers placed back to back (Figure 5).

IO. Poke pin in the top of the hat.

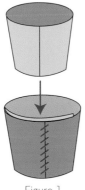

Figure 1

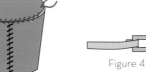

Figure 2

Figure 3

Figure 4

Figure 5

tip: *Can't find shamrock stickers? You can use a heart-shaped punch and gold sticker paper (such as office supply labels) instead. Four hearts attached at the center with glue form a shamrock.*

End of the Rainbow Tablecloth

Not everything at a St. Patrick's Day party has to be green. This two-piece tablecloth, with its light blue top overlay and green striped skirt, provides just enough contrast to give the other decorations a place to shine. Rainbow-colored ribbons gather up the ruched corners for a custom fit. The instructions here will work for any rectangular or square table.

FINISHED SIZE:
Customized for your table

44

Materials and Supplies

Measure your table's length, width, and height, and use the formulas in Calculating the Yardage (page 47) to determine how much of each fabric to buy.

- **Green striped fabric:** for the table skirt

- **White cotton fabric:** for the table top

- **Blue cotton fabric:** for the tablecloth overlay and facings

- **Ribbon:** ⅛" wide in green, light green, blue, and yellow (6 pieces of each color cut to 20" lengths)

- **Bodkin**

- **Tailor's chalk**

INSTRUCTIONS

The table skirt is attached to a plain white cotton top, which will be hidden beneath the light blue tablecloth overlay. The ruched effect on the overlay corners is achieved by sewing on facings that become channels for the ribbons; pulling the ribbons ruches the fabric.

Table Skirt

1. Create a rolled machine hem, as described in Edge and Seam Finishes (page 154), along a long edge of the green striped fabric, and refer to Gathers and Ruffles (page 156) to gather the opposite long edge.

2. Leaving the first 2" free, pin the gathered edge of the table skirt around all 4 sides of the white cotton table top piece with right sides together. Leave extra gathers around each of the corners so the tablecloth will lie flat when turned (Figure 1). When you reach the end of the gathered fabric, leave a 2" margin unattached.

3. Stitch the tablecloth skirt to the top along all 4 edges using a ½" seam allowance.

4. Pin the free sides of the skirt fabric together, and stitch using a ½" seam allowance (Figure 2). Press the seam open, and follow the instructions in Clean-Finish Seam (page 154) to create a neatly finished seam.

5. Stitch the remaining length of the table skirt to the top (Figure 3). Trim the seam to ⅝" and overcast the raw edges using a zigzag stitch.

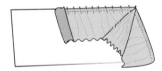

Figure 1

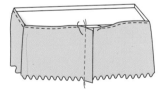

Figure 2

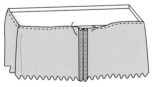

Figure 3

Tablecloth Overlay

I. Lay the overlay fabric over the table, right side *down*, and arrange it so it is evenly draped over the table. The overlay should hang over the edges by 10″ on all sides. Working on a corner at a time, pinch out a triangle of folded fabric, pin, and mark with tailor's chalk. Stitch on the chalk line (Figure 4). Trim away the excess fabric (Figure 5). Repeat with the remaining corners.

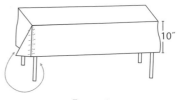

Figure 4

2. Turn the overlay right side out and press.

3. Fold the bottom edge toward the wrong side ¼″ and press. Fold again ¼″ and press. Topstitch in place to create a hem.

4. To create facings for the ruched corners, cut 4 strips 2½″ × 10″. Fold the strips in half lengthwise, right sides together, and stitch the long edge and a short end using a ¼″ seam allowance (Figure 6). Clip corners, turn, and press. Fold the raw edge of the tube under ¼″, and topstitch to close. Repeat to create 4 facings.

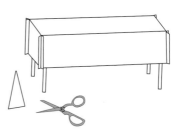

Figure 5

5. Turn the overlay wrong side out and place it over the table. Pin a facing to each corner so that the bottom edge of the facing is even with the bottom edge of the overlay and the sides of the facing lie evenly on either side of the corner seam. Stitch along either side of the facing ⅛″ from the edge. Sew another seam down the center of the facing (in the corner seam of the overlay), splitting the facing into 2 even channels (Figure 7).

Figure 6

6. Using a bodkin, feed 3 ribbons through each channel on the tablecloth. Knot 6 ribbons together at the top of each facing. (This will allow you to remove the ribbons to launder the overlay if needed.) Turn the overlay right side out, and cinch and tie the ribbons on each of the 4 corners.

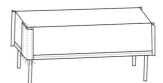

Figure 7

tip: *Table shapes can vary. If the cinched corners of the table-cloth are drooping, find four boxes and use packing tape to attach a box at each corner of the table under the tablecloth. This will create just enough shape for the tablecloth to sit squarely.*

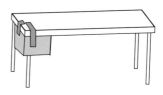

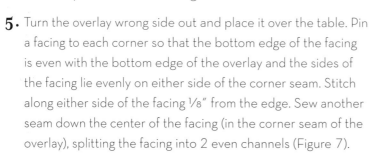
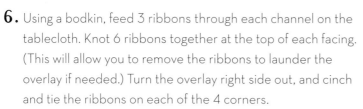

CALCULATING THE YARDAGE

Table Top

To calculate length: length of table (a) ___ + 1" = ___

To calculate width: width of table (c) ___ + 1" = ___

Table Skirt

To calculate length:

length of table (a) ___ × 2 = ___ (d)

width of table (c) ___ × 2 = ___ (e)

Add (d) ___ + (e) ___ = ____ × 1.5 = ____

To calculate width: height of table (b) ___ + 1" = ___

If the stripes on the fabric run vertically from selvage to selvage, you will need to sew multiple panels of fabric together to get the needed length. Use a clean-finish seam (page 154) to join panels.

Tablecloth Overlay

To calculate length: length of table (a) ___ + 21" = ___

To calculate width: width of table (c) ___ + 21" = ___

For a 24"-wide table, if the fabric is 44"-45" wide, simply cut the fabric to the length required and leave the selvages untouched.

For the ruched corners, use 4 pieces of fabric measuring 2½" × 10" for the facings.

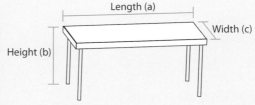

Rich Truffles

All of this talk of hidden pots of gold reminded us of another favorite treasure—the truffle. Is there any dessert more decadent and sought after than a creamy filling smothered in smooth chocolate? We offer recipes for two scrumptious truffle fillings—Mint Cookies-and-Cream and Raspberry Buttercream. Make one, or make both!

INGREDIENTS

Each recipe makes 35 truffles.

Mint Cookies-and-Cream Truffles

1 package cream-filled
chocolate sandwich cookies

1–2 teaspoons mint (or spearmint) extract

8 oz. cream cheese (at room temperature)

2 packages (12 oz. each)
white chocolate chips

1 package (12 oz.) semisweet chocolate chips

Raspberry Truffles

4–8 cups powdered sugar

½ cup unsalted butter (1 stick),
at room temperature

½ cup frozen raspberries (thawed)

1 teaspoon vanilla extract

A few tablespoons whole milk

1 package (12 oz.) semisweet chocolate chips

6 oz. white chocolate chips

Red food color

DIRECTIONS

You will need a wax paper—lined baking sheet (or some flat plates) that will fit in your refrigerator. You'll also need a piping bag. If you don't have one, use a thick plastic food storage bag with the bottom corner snipped to the size you need.

Prepare the fillings (at right) and place them on baking sheets in the refrigerator as directed in the individual recipes. Chill in the refrigerator for 15 minutes. Roll the chilled fillings between your palms to form smooth balls; then return them to the refrigerator for another 15—30 minutes.

To prepare the coating, microwave the chocolate chips on full power for 10-second intervals, stirring after every interval, until they are melted. The total time will vary depending on the microwave. (You may use a double boiler if you prefer.)

To coat the truffles, spear a chilled ball of filling on a fork and dip it into the melted chocolate so that it is completely covered. Remove, and use a second fork to slide it back onto the wax paper. Repeat this process with all the truffles. If the filling is showing through, apply a second coat of chocolate. If the chocolate starts to harden as you are working, just microwave it again for 10 seconds.

Place the coated truffles on a baking sheet in the refrigerator for 5—10 minutes to harden.

To decorate the truffles, melt the decorating chocolate. Use a small piping tip to drizzle it in a zigzag motion over the truffles. Work from the front to the back of each truffle. After you've done all the truffles, rotate the baking sheet and repeat the zigzag design going front to back.

Store the truffles in an airtight container in the refrigerator.

MINT COOKIES-AND-CREAM *Filling:* Crush the **cream-filled chocolate sandwich cookies** in a plastic bag using a rolling pin. Using a fork, combine the cookies with the **mint or spearmint extract** and the **cream cheese** in a large bowl until it forms a thick paste and is uniformly dark brown. Drop the filling by quarter-size balls onto a wax paper—lined baking sheet and chill as directed in the main recipe.

Coating: Melt the **white chocolate chips,** and follow the main recipe instructions to form and coat the truffles. Melt the **semisweet chocolate chips** and use to decorate the truffles.

RASPBERRY *Filling:* Use a mixer to combine the **unsalted butter** with 1 cup of powdered sugar. Add a **second cup of powdered sugar** and mix until smooth. Add the remaining **2 cups of powdered sugar,** the **frozen raspberries,** and the **vanilla extract.** Mix on medium speed to a toothpaste consistency. *If the filling is too thin, add* **another cup of powdered sugar.** *If it's too thick and hard to mix, add* **milk,** *1 tablespoon at a time, until it reaches proper consistency.* Drop the filling in quarter-size balls onto a wax paper—lined baking sheet and chill as directed in the main recipe.

Coating: Melt the **semisweet chocolate chips,** and follow the main recipe instructions to form and coat the truffles. Melt the **white chocolate chips** and add **red food coloring** to make the melted chocolate pink; use it to decorate the truffles.

BRIDAL SHOWER

An engagement is a time to celebrate—not just the upcoming wedding, but also the bride-to-be herself. For an intimate bridal shower brunch, we decided to revel in feminine details. We wanted flowers, wedding rings, tiers of ruffles, and white! After all, why should the bride have all the fun?

Although the party looks elegant, the materials could not be more humble. The focal point is the giant fabric flowers. They make a bold statement and a lovely prop for photographs.

It's hard not to feel beautiful when you are holding them. The ruffled tablecloth is inspired by frilly, frothy wedding dresses.

At a bridal shower, no one wants to be without a ring, so we tied inexpensive toy versions to each of the napkins with ribbon. We sewed up simple gift boxes, which serve as both favors and place cards. Pattern and texture are introduced through the damask-patterned plates and "chargers" cut from fancy scrapbook papers. Homemade petit fours make for a sweet finish to an exquisite event.

Fabric Flowers

Inspired by oversized paper flowers, we decided to come up with a fabric version. We studied some real-life flowers and modeled our pattern after them. Try making one to learn the technique, and then queue up an assembly line to create your own personal garden.

FINISHED SIZE: 12″ wide

Materials and Supplies

Yardages are based on 44″-wide fabric. Makes 1 flower.

- Muslin: 1½ yards (bleached or unbleached)

- Interfacing: 1½ yards fusible interfacing (45″ wide), such as Pellon Decor-Bond

- Elastic bands or small ponytail holders: 3

- White bias tape: 12″ piece (or use ½″-wide ribbon)

Cutting

The template patterns are on pullout page P1. Enlarge 200%.

Muslin:
Cut 10 small and 10 large petals using the template patterns.

Fusible interfacing:
Cut 10 small and 10 large petals using the dashed lines on the template patterns.

INSTRUCTIONS

1. Follow the manufacturer's directions to fuse the interfacing to the muslin pieces.

2. Arrange petals in stacks of 2 with right sides together. Sew each petal along the edge of the interfacing, leaving the base of the petal open. Clip the tip, turn, and press.

tip: *Use a short stitch length so you can turn the petals with more force. Use a chopstick or other long, blunt object to smooth open the seams. There is no need to spend time clipping curves. Simply clip the tip where the petal comes to a point.*

3. Take a small petal in your hands and roll it into a long tube shape (Figure 1). Wrap an end with an elastic band to secure it (Figure 2).

4. Take a second small petal and wrap it around the center (Figure 3). Gradually add the 3 additional small petals, alternating sides. Secure with another elastic band (Figures 4 and 5).

tip: *It can take a few tries to get a nice flower shape. Don't worry if the petals are becoming wrinkled. Simply iron them flat and start again. The more you work them in your hands, the better they will retain their flower shape. Pinch them tight around the base of the flower and fan them open as you work.*

5. Repeat Step 4 with the large petals. Gather up 5 large petals in your hands, a petal at a time, and secure with an elastic band.

6. Insert the flower center you made in Step 4 into the center of the larger petals (Figure 6).

7. Fluff and arrange the petals, folding them down to have a nice, open flower shape (Figure 7).

8. Wrap the base of the flower with a ribbon or white bias tape to hide the elastic band (Figure 8).

Figure 1

Figure 2

Figure 3

Figure 4

Figure 5

Figure 6

Figure 7

Figure 8

spring

Ruffled Tablecloth

The ruffled tiers on this tablecloth require more patience than skill, but we think the finished product is worth the extra time. The inexpensive materials and straightforward construction are very forgiving, so please don't get too caught up in the math. Try to purchase the widest fabric you can find to save yourself time when cutting and piecing the strips.

FINISHED SIZE:
105½" diameter (fits table 48" diameter × 28¾" high)

To fit this tablecloth base and ruffles to a different size table, refer to Round Tables (page 157).

Materials and Supplies

- White cotton fabric:

  108″ wide: 3 yards for tablecloth (If using a smaller-width fabric, buy enough to piece together a 108″ × 108″ square.)

  120″ wide: 3¼ yards for ruffles

- Unbleached muslin: 44″ wide, 1¾ yards

- Eyelet trim: *Narrow:* 1½″ wide, 10 yards (7 yards if pregathered); *Wide:* 5″ wide, 12 yards (8 yards if pregathered)

- Tailor's chalk or removable marker

- String: 2 yards

Cutting

White cotton tablecloth fabric:

  Cut a circle 101½″ in diameter for the tablecloth base.*

White cotton ruffle fabric:

  Cut 5 strips 5″ × width of fabric; join end to end.

  Cut 5 strips 10½″ × width of fabric; join end to end.

  Cut 4 strips 6½″ × width of fabric; join end to end.

Unbleached muslin:

  Cut 12 strips 4 ¾″ × width of fabric; join end to end.

* To draw and cut out, refer to Drafting a Large Circle (page 157).

INSTRUCTIONS

This tablecloth starts with a plain base, to which you attach the tiers of ruffles.

I. Fold the strips of fabric lengthwise, and use the instructions in Gathers and Ruffles (page 156) to gather them into ruffles along the raw edges. The first ruffle (Step 2) should measure 319″ long once it has been gathered. Each subsequent ruffle added will need to be a little shorter than the previous ruffle. Adjust the length as you are pinning it to the tablecloth base.

2. Pin the gathered edge of the narrowest white ruffle around the perimeter of the tablecloth and sew in place using a ½″ seam allowance. Trim the seam to ³⁄₈″ to neaten the edges, and press.

tip: *If you plan to use and launder the tablecloth frequently, we recommend finishing all seams with a three-step zigzag (if your machine has it) or a regular zigzag to minimize raveling of the raw edges. Press, and topstitch the ruffles in place.*

3. Using tailor's chalk or a removable marker, mark a line 4½" above (inside) the first ruffle all the way around the circumference of the tablecloth. Pin the widest white ruffle upside down along the line and stitch it in place using a ³⁄₈" seam allowance.

4. Sew the unbleached muslin ruffle 2" above (inside) the last ruffle as in Step 3.

5. Sew the wide eyelet trim 4½" above the sewn edge of the unbleached muslin ruffle.

6. Sew the medium-width white ruffle 2½" above the seamline of the eyelet trim.

7. Finish by sewing the narrow eyelet trim just above the ruffle added in Step 6 so it overlaps the ruffle below it.

8. Press all ruffles toward the bottom edge.

Everyone loves taking home a present. These little gift boxes allow you to personalize your table with any color scheme and fabric you choose. Tuck a small favor inside, such as chocolates.

FINISHED SIZE: 2½" × 2½" × 2½"

Materials and Supplies

Makes 1 box.

- Satin or cotton sateen fabric: ½ yard peach or buff

- Interfacing:
  ¼ yard heavy-duty interfacing (20" wide), such as Pellon Peltex 70 Ultra-Firm Stabilizer

  ¼ yard lightweight fusible interfacing (20" wide), such as Pellon 911FF Fusible Featherweight

- Silver cord or ribbon:
  1 yard, ⅛" wide

Cutting

Heavy-duty interfacing:
  Cut 7 squares 2½" × 2½".
  Cut 2 rectangles 1¼" × 2½".

Lightweight fusible interfacing:
  Cut 1 strip 3" × 10½".
  Cut 1 strip 3" × 13".

Silver cord or ribbon:
  Cut 2 pieces 18" long.

Folded Fabric Gift Box

INSTRUCTIONS

I. Leaving a margin of at least 6" from the edges of the peach fabric, place the squares and rectangles of heavy-duty interfacing on the wrong side of the fabric to form a cross (Figure 1). Center the 3" × 10½" strips of lightweight fusible interfacing over the vertical part of the cross. Place the 3" × 13" lightweight fusible interfacing over the horizontal portion of the cross (Figure 2). Fuse all pieces in place.

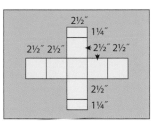

Figure 1

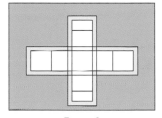

Figure 2

2. With right sides together, place the cross on another layer of peach fabric and cut out, leaving a generous ¼" seam allowance.

3. Insert silver ribbon between the layers along short ends of the cross (Figure 3).

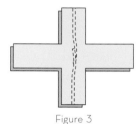

Figure 3

4. Using a very short stitch length (1.5mm), stitch along the outside edge of the heavy-duty interfacing, leaving a 3" gap along a side as shown (Figure 4). Clip all corners, turn, and press.

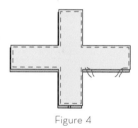

Figure 4

5. Fold in the raw edges of the opening and pin. Topstitch all the way around the cross ⅛" from the edge.

6. Fold the cross into a box shape, pressing each fold to give it shape. It may help to place a small cardboard or ring box in the middle as a mold. Tie the ribbon in a bow, adding a name tag as desired.

REBECCA'S RECIPE:

Petit Fours

Handmade Hostess

Petit fours conjure up images of elegant parties, ladies' brunches, and high teas. Although they look fancy, these tiny cakes are actually quite simple to make. Use your favorite yellow (or pound) cake recipe or use the one for Witch and Monster Cupcakes (page 136). If you are rushed for time, you can pick up a presliced loaf of pound cake at the bakery and no one will know the difference.

INGREDIENTS

Makes approximately 24.

*Prepared pound cake
baked in a square pan*

Buttercream Icing (recipe follows):

  *1 cup unsalted butter
  (2 sticks), softened*

  8 cups powdered sugar

  ¼–¾ cup whole milk

  2 teaspoons vanilla extract

  ½ cup cocoa powder (optional)

Fondant (You can substitute
melted chocolate chips.)*

** Available at craft and baking
supply stores; some types come
premixed and precolored.*

tip: To make a chocolate
buttercream, substitute ½ cup
of cocoa powder for the vanilla
extract.

DIRECTIONS

You will need a 1˝ square cookie cutter or a knife, a tiny flower cookie cutter, and a rolling pin.

Cut the cake into ¼˝-thick slices. Cut the slices into 1˝ squares using a square cookie cutter or a knife. Layer Buttercream Icing between 2 squares of cake. Take a piece of fondant and roll it out ⅛˝–¼˝ thick on a smooth surface lightly covered with powdered sugar. Lay it on top of the cake and gently wrap and press it around each petit four. Trim excess fondant from the corners and bottom with kitchen shears. Use the tiny flower cookie cutter to cut small flowers out of the fondant. Adhere them to the tops of the petit fours with a drop of water.

To make chocolate-covered petit fours instead, melt chocolate chips in a microwave-safe bowl. Put the prepared cakes on a wire rack on top of a baking sheet, and gently pour melted chocolate over them. Any excess chocolate will be caught on the sheet and can be scraped off and remelted.

BUTTERCREAM ICING Combine the **unsalted butter, powdered sugar, milk,*** and **vanilla extract.** Mix with an electric mixer until thick but spreadable. The buttercream should have the consistency of toothpaste.

* Start with the smallest amount of milk, and adjust as you mix to create a spreadable consistency.

EXTRA TOUCH

To make the parasol backdrop, we used PVC pipe to build a stand approximately 6' wide × 6½' tall × 7" deep. We wrapped it with a tarp, front and back. We cut slits in both layers of the tarp and inserted parasols purchased from Luna Bazaar (see Resources, page 158). The handles of the parasols rest in the slits in both the front and back tarps for stability.

JAPANESE GARDEN PARTY

Our love of Japanese gardens was the jumping-off point for this garden party. A few special projects take center stage, while details such as place settings, tablecloths, and flowers are simple but generous. Gold Chiavari chairs are tied with handmade obi chair wraps. A bowl of peonies and cabbage roses leaves room above for a lantern made of mitsumata branches and twinkle lights. Brightly colored parasols in fresh spring colors create a vibrant backdrop.

There is an abundance of Asian-inspired party accessories available now—takeout boxes you could wrap with ribbon, beautiful chopsticks, lanterns, parasols, and fans. Some of these would make lovely favors for your guests. However there is no need to crowd your table with too many themed items. As you plan your own party, be sure to provide places where your guests can admire the garden venue itself or the simplicity of a freshly cut strawberry without any additional adornment. Which aspects of the party will you create and where you will you allow nature to speak for itself?

Obi Chair Wraps

These chair wraps, sewn from vibrant brocade fabrics, are inspired by the sashes on traditional Japanese dress. The instructions will work for a standard Chiavari chair with a 15″-wide back but could easily be adjusted for a similar seat you already have on hand. You may need to adjust the length of the fabric strips and the placement of the buttonhole. This project is easier if you have a chair on hand for fittings while you sew.

FINISHED SIZE:
5¾″ × 43″

Materials and Supplies

Makes 1 obi wrap.

- Blue brocade fabric: ½ yard
  (at least 45″ wide)

- Green brocade fabric: ¼ yard
  (at least 45″ wide)

- Green ribbon: ⅝″ wide, 1½ yards

- Blue ribbon: ¼″ wide, 1 yard for loops
  (optional)

- Tear-away stabilizer: 1½″ × 1½″
  for buttonhole

Cutting

- Blue brocade fabric: Cut 2 strips
  6½″ × width of fabric.*

- Green brocade fabric: Cut 1 strip
  4½″ × width of fabric.*

- Green ribbon: Cut 2 pieces 23″ long.

- Blue ribbon: Cut 2 pieces 13″ long.

** If the fabric is 45″ wide, do not trim this
strip to 44¼″ just yet. This will give you
one less fraying edge to deal with.*

tip: *Brocade is prone to heavy fraying, so
make sure the cuts are clean (use a fresh rotary
blade or sharp scissors). Handle the fabric as little
as possible once it's been cut, and when you sew,
use a shorter-than-usual stitch length (1.8mm). Be
gentle when turning the piece.*

INSTRUCTIONS

1. Fold the green strip in half lengthwise with right sides together, and sew the longest edge using a ¼″ seam allowance. Turn right side out gently and press.

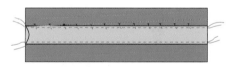

Figure 1

2. Lay the green strip on top of a blue piece of fabric, lining up the centers, and pin in place. Topstitch in place using a ⅛″ seam allowance (Figure 1).

3. Refer to Figure 2 to center the ⅝″-wide ribbons on either end of the obi, and baste in place using a ⅛″ seam allowance. Baste the 13″ loops of narrow ribbon at the top of the obi approximately 15½″ from either end as shown. The ribbon loops are optional but helpful if the obi is made from slippery fabric. We learned (the hard way) that these loops will prevent the obi from sliding down the chair.

Figure 2

4. Lay the remaining piece of blue fabric on top of the obi, right sides together, and stitch around the top, bottom, and a side using a ¼″ seam allowance (Figure 3).

Figure 3

5. Turn right side out and press. Do not clip corners. Instead, use a chopstick or point turner to gently turn the corners.

6. Fold the raw edges under ¼" and topstitch in place.

7. Sew a ¾" buttonhole in the center of the obi 15½" from the edge that is not topstitched. Cut a small piece of tear-away stabilizer and lay it beneath the fabric as you stitch the buttonhole. Remove stabilizer once the buttonhole is complete. To cut down on fraying when you open the buttonhole, choose a buttonhole that leaves extra cutting space if your machine provides that option.

8. Wrap the obi around the chair as shown (Figure 4).

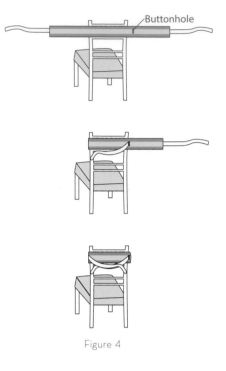

Figure 4

tip: *To provide an extra pop of color on the table, sew leftover pieces of brocade into strips and layer them between the plates.*

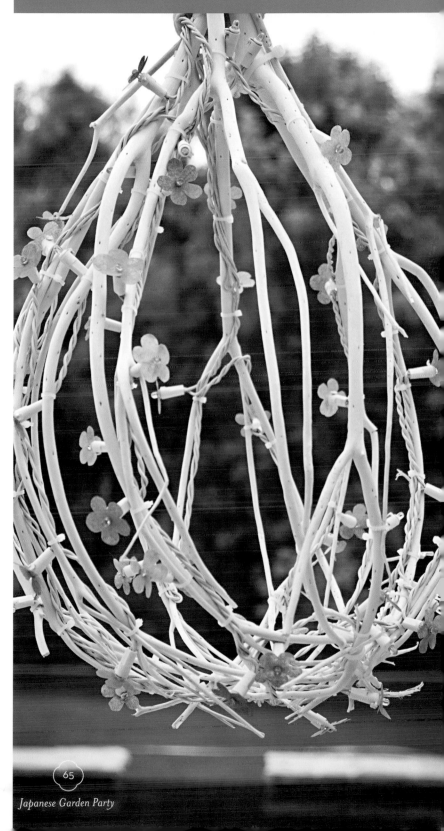

Cherry Blossom Lantern

The cherry blossom lantern looks complicated to make, but it is actually quite simple. The secret lies in the mitsumata branches themselves. When soaked in water, they become pliable, allowing you to shape them into this beautiful dewdrop shape.

FINISHED SIZE: Approximately 20" wide × 30" tall

Materials and Supplies

Resources (page 158) lists vendors for some of these materials.

- Lutradur Mixed Media Sheets: regular (70 gram), 2 sheets, 8½" × 11"

- Pink acrylic paint

- Sponge paintbrush and water

- Hole punch

- Mitsumata branches: 6–8

- Large inflatable ball: 15" diameter

- Zip ties: at least 30 each of medium (7") and small (4")

- LED twinkle lights: 70-bulb strand with white cord

- White extension cord

- Cream-colored yarn, rope, or decorative ribbon: to wrap stem

- Craft knife or small hand-held saw (*optional*)

INSTRUCTIONS

Making the Blossoms

The template pattern is on pullout page P2.

1. Cover a work surface with plastic sheeting or work outside on the grass. Using the sponge brush and a cup full of water, paint the Lutradur sheets with pink paint. Dip the brush in water first, dab it into the pink paint, and then lightly wash the Lutradur with color. The more water on the brush, the lighter the color will be. Allow the Lutradur to dry. For more Lutradur tips, see *Fabulous Fabric Art with Lutradur* by Lesley Riley (from C&T Publishing).

2. Trace the cherry blossom template pattern onto the Lutradur and cut out 70 cherry blossoms (or use a blossom-shaped punch to speed this along).

3. Punch a hole at the center of each blossom for a light bulb. Fold each petal gently toward the center and set aside.

Shaping the Branches

1. Fill a bathtub or other large container with water and allow the mitsumata branches to soak for at least an hour (and up to overnight). You can wet an old towel to weight them down so they are totally submerged.

2. Protect the floor with towels if needed. Select a branch with a sturdy stem, and wrap it around the inflatable ball. You will need to hold the branch in place with your hand until you have secured it with a zip tie. (The branch will not magically stay there!) The first 2 branches are the most unwieldy, but after you have a basic structure, the rest will go quickly. Select a second branch, and wrap it around the opposite side, allowing the tips of the branches to meet in the center. Secure with zip ties, using medium ties for the thick portion of the stem and small ties for the delicate branches at the end.

tip: *Test one of the twinkle light bulbs to make sure the hole you have punched is the correct size. You may need to use a smaller hole punch if the bulbs are very small. If the bulb is only slightly bigger than the opening, you can gently force it into place.*

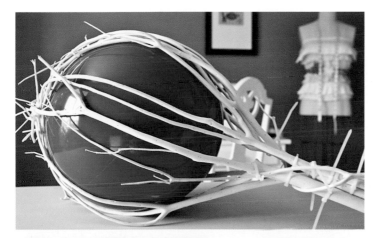

Attaching the Lights

1. Make sure that the branches are completely dry before attaching the lights. Beginning at the top and making every effort to hide the wires, wrap the lights around the branches and secure with small zip ties. This step may be easier if you hang the lantern from a length of string and work on it while standing up. Trim the zip ties.

2. Place the Lutradur cherry blossoms onto the lights.

3. Attach the extension cord to the twinkle lights. Wrap the top of the lantern with the rope, heavy yarn, or ribbon to disguise the cord's plug, and tie off the end.

3. Continue wrapping branches until you have even coverage around the surface of the ball. Let dry overnight.

4. Deflate the ball and remove it from the branches.

tip: *If you don't like the shape that you created, remove the zip ties and resoak the branches for an hour. They will be supple again and ready to reshape.*

Lotus Blossom Place Cards

Brianna

These lotus blossoms are not only place cards but also miniature works of art. Each of your guests can take a little bit of the garden home. We think you will find this project simpler than origami and every bit as elegant.

FINISHED SIZE: 6" × 6"

Materials and Supplies

- Heavy white paper: for blossoms

- Yellow paper: for inner
  and outer centers

- Yellow brads

INSTRUCTIONS

*The template patterns are on
pullout page P1. Enlarge flower
template patterns 200%. Inner
and outer center template patterns
do not need to be enlarged.*

1. For each flower, cut each of the
4 blossoms from heavy white paper
using the template patterns.

2. Cut 2 circles out of the yellow
paper using the inner and outer
center template patterns.

3. Make fringe cuts around the outside
of the yellow circles using the markings on the template patterns as a
guide. Fold the fringe up toward the
center to form the stamens.

4. Stack the shapes, aligning the
centers, and push a brad through
the center.

5. Use the side of a pencil to gently
curve the petals toward the center.

Bento Box Desserts

Everything about this party felt airy and springlike, and I wanted the desserts to have that same feel. Making several bite-sized desserts sounds like work, but the trick is to keep some of them very simple and rely on presentation to do the rest. On an elegant divided plate, moist, light macaroons are combined with store-bought cakes and a fresh strawberry for a pleasing arrangement that only looks complex.

INGREDIENTS

Makes 24 cookies.

Vanilla cake and chocolate cake (purchased)

Buttercream Icing (use the recipe in Petit Fours, page 59)

Coconut Macaroons (recipe follows):

2 egg whites

⅛ teaspoon salt

2 teaspoons vanilla extract

½ teaspoon almond extract

½ cup sweetened condensed milk

1 package (14 oz.) shredded coconut (approximately 5½ cups)

Fresh strawberries

Purchased raspberry puree (optional)

DIRECTIONS

You will need a 1½˝ square cookie cutter or a knife, a baking sheet, and a nonstick baking mat (such as Silpat) or parchment paper. To pipe buttercream onto the cakes, you will need a piping bag or a plastic food storage bag with the bottom corner snipped to the size you need.

Cut the vanilla and chocolate cakes into 1½˝ cubes, using the cookie cutter or a knife. Pipe on a dollop of Buttercream Icing. To make the macaroons "pop" on the plate, set them in a little pool of raspberry puree. Place half a fresh strawberry on each plate.

COCONUT MACAROONS   Using a whisk attachment on your mixer, whip 2 **egg whites** until the peaks are firm. Add the **salt, vanilla extract,** and **almond extract,** and whisk together. Add the **sweetened condensed milk** and **shredded coconut.** Stir until thoroughly combined. Drop spoon-sized balls of the mixture onto the paper-covered baking sheet. Bake at 325°F for 10 minutes or until the edges of the macaroons turn golden. Let them cool on the pan.

PIXIE PARTY

A little girl's wishes for her birthday party can be precious and vexing at the same time. "You want *what* kind of party?" we ask nervously. Those of us who love creating are thrilled to have an excuse to use our talents. When else can we buy yards and yards of tulle or make woodland wreaths for all of the guests to wear?

Our guest of honor wanted to see where the pixies live. We recreated the pixies' home complete with mushroom stools. A giant leaf adorns the tablecloth, giving the impression that the table is one big, fluffy flower. Our pixies snacked on lavender and purple *macaron* "mushrooms."

The wood cake stands are inexpensive, DIY versions of fancier displays we've seen in stores. We purchased wood circles at the craft store, and the bases are wrapped in a heavy paper that looks like bark. A little moss, a toadstool, and a small arrangement of fresh flowers complete the décor.

We wanted our guests to feel just as special as the birthday girl, so we invited everyone to dress up for the event. Each guest took a pixie dust pouch home so she can always find her way back to the land of the fairies.

Tutu Tablecloth

We created a gentle ombré effect by selecting several shades of purple and lavender tulle. We expect this tablecloth to be in regular rotation long after the party, so we made the green top and leaf removable so it can be easily washed.

FINISHED SIZE:
Fits table 31″ diameter × 21″ high

Materials and Supplies

- Light lavender tulle: 1½ yards (We used a sparkle mesh.)

- Medium lavender tulle: 2¼ yards

- Lavender tulle: 4½ yards

- Purple tulle: 4½ yards

- White cotton or muslin: 1 yard for top

- Purple sateen: 2¼ yards for table skirt

- Green sateen: 2⅛ yards for table top and leaf

- Cotton cord: ⅛″ wide, 3¼ yards

- Interfacing: ½ yard fusible fleece interfacing (44″ wide)

- Button: clear plastic, 1″

- Bodkin

- Tailor's chalk

Cutting

The template pattern is on pullout page P1. Enlarge 200%.

Light lavender tulle:

Cut 3 strips 12½″ × 1½ yards.

Medium lavender tulle:

Cut 2 strips 22½″ × 2¼ yards.

Lavender tulle:

Cut 1 strip 32½″ × 4½ yards.

Purple tulle:

Cut 1 strip 43″ × 4½ yards.

White cotton:

Cut 1 circle 32″ in diameter (see Tip, at right).

Purple sateen:

Cut 2 strips 22″ × 2¼ yards.

Green sateen:

Cut 1 circle 32″ in diameter (see Tip below).

Cut 1 bias strip 6½″ × 2⅞ yards.*

Fusible fleece interfacing:

Cut 2 pixie leaves using the template pattern.

* See Continuous Bias Trim (page 156) for instructions.

tip: *Most child-sized tables are lightweight enough that you can flip them over and trace the tabletop directly onto the fabric with chalk. Use a ruler to add a ½″ seam allowance all the way around the circumference. Alternatively, refer to Drafting a Large Circle (page 157).*

INSTRUCTIONS

Sewing the Leaf

1. Follow the manufacturer's directions to fuse the fusible fleece pixie leaves to the wrong side of the green sateen. Cut around the leaves, leaving a rough ½″ seam allowance.

2. Place the leaves right sides together and pin, leaving the bottom of the leaf open. Sew, using a short stitch length, along the edge of the fleece interfacing.

3. Turn and press. Fold in the raw edge along the bottom of the leaf and topstitch closed.

4. Decorate the leaf with topstitching. See photo (at right) for guidance. Sew approximately ½″ in from the edge and create a channel up the center to serve as the central vein.

5. Approximately ½″ from the center of the base of the leaf, sew a buttonhole wide enough to accommodate the button.

Sewing the Table Top

1. Fold the green sateen bias strip in half with wrong sides together. Pin it to the right side of the green circle all the way around with raw edges aligned, leaving the ends unattached. Sew using a ½" seam allowance.

2. When you reach the beginning of the circle, stitch the loose ends together, leaving a ½" gap in the middle of the seam near the fold to feed the cord through. Finish stitching the bias trim around the circle.

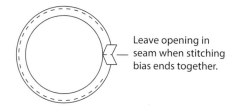

Leave opening in seam when stitching bias ends together.

3. Trim seam allowance to ⅜" and finish with a 3-step zigzag if your machine has it, or a regular zigzag.

4. Sew a channel ⅜" from the folded edge of the bias tape. Using a bodkin, feed the cord through the channel and knot the ends together. The cord will be cinched around the table to secure.

5. Attach the clear button 1½" from the lower edge of the inside of the bias strip, on the opposite side from the channel opening.

Sewing the Tablecloth

1. Sew the 3 strips of light lavender tulle end to end to create a strip 12½" × 4½ yards.

2. Sew the 2 strips of medium lavender tulle end to end to create a strip 22½" × 4½ yards.

3. Fold the strips of tulle (all 4 colors) in half lengthwise. Stack the tulle with the folded edges aligned, with the purple tulle on the bottom, then the lavender, the medium lavender, and finally the light lavender on top. Pin the folded edges together. Baste ¼" from the folds and gather until the unit measures approximately 100" in length.

4. Pin the gathered tulle around the outer edge of the white cotton circle, raw edges aligned, with the light lavender ruffle facing the right side of the white cotton, adjusting the gathers to fit. Stitch, using a ½" seam allowance. Trim ruffles to neaten edges. Set aside.

5. To create the underskirt, refer to Clean-Finish Seam (page 154) to sew the 2 strips of purple sateen end to end. Hem a long edge and both short sides of the fabric using a ¼" rolled machine hem as described in Edge and Seam Finishes (page 154).

6. Baste the long raw edge of the purple sateen ¼" from the edge and pull threads to gather until it is approximately 100" long.

7. Place the white cotton circle right side up on a flat surface (ruffles will be on top). With the right side of the purple sateen facing the ruffles and with right sides together, pin and sew the raw edge of the purple sateen around the outer circumference of the white cotton circle using a ¼" seam allowance.

Pixie Dust Pouch

These pixie dust pouches are a cinch to make, and perfect for holding tiny treasures. They're so charming, sewn in a beautiful mix of linen and silk, that we recommend making a few extras for yourself.

FINISHED SIZE:
4½" wide × 5" tall

Materials and Supplies

Makes 1 pouch.

- Linen: ⅔ yard for exterior

- Lavender silk: ⅔ yard for interior

- Gold cord: ⅛" wide, 1 yard

- Gold leather: 4" × 5" (see Resources, page 158); alternatively, you may use faux leather, such as Leatherette

- Bodkin

Cutting

The template pattern is on pullout page P2.

Linen:
Cut 1 circle 16½"
in diameter.*

Lavender silk:
Cut 1 circle 16½"
in diameter.*

Gold leather:
Cut 2 leaves using the
template pattern.

* To draw and cut out, refer to Drafting a Large Circle (page 157).

INSTRUCTIONS

1. Sew a size 10 (½") buttonhole in the linen fabric 1¾" from and parallel to the edge.

2. Place the 2 fabric circles right sides together and sew around the outer edge, using a ³⁄₈" seam allowance and leaving a 2" opening.

3. Turn the piece right side out, and press well. Fold the raw edges under along the opening and pin. Topstitch around the entire outer edge using a ¼" seam allowance.

4. To create the channel for the gold cord, first stitch around the circle 1" from the outside edge. Sew another circle 1⅞" from the outside edge. The buttonhole from Step 1 should lie between these 2 rows of stitching.

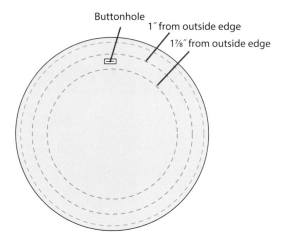

Buttonhole

1" from outside edge

1⅞" from outside edge

5. Use a bodkin to feed the gold cord through the channel. Fill the bag with treasures, tie the cord into a bow, and trim the ends to the desired length.

6. About 1" from an end, tie the cord into a knot, slip on the gold leaf, and tie again to secure. Repeat for the other end.

Handmade Hostess

Mushroom Stool

The lush velvet fabric on the top of this mushroom stool makes a cushy place for tired pixies to sit. The base is sewn from heavily interfaced linen. If you are comfortable using a staple gun, you should have no trouble upholstering the top.

FINISHED SIZE:
12" wide × 12" tall

Materials and Supplies

- Maroon velvet: 1 yard for top

- Linen: ²/₃ yard for base

- Interfacing: ¹/₂ yard heavy-duty fusible interfacing (20″ wide), such as Pellon Peltex 71F Single-Sided Fusible Ultra-Firm Stabilizer

- White felt: 8¹/₂″ × 11″

- Buttons: 3 leather-wrapped buttons, 1″ diameter

- Gold elastic cord: ¹/₂ yard

- Foam: 2″ thick, 14″ × 28″

- Hot glue gun

- Staple gun and staples

- Serrated knife or scissors: to trim foam

- Unfinished wooden stool *

Our four-legged wooden stool measured approximately 11″ diameter × 8″ tall. If your stool's measurements vary, you may need to adjust the height and width of the bottom wrap as well as the amount of foam.

Cutting

Linen: Cut 2 pieces 8¹/₂″ × 34″.

Heavy-duty fusible interfacing:
    Cut 2 pieces 8″ × 16³/₄″.

White felt:
    Cut 3 circles 3¹/₂″ in diameter.*

Gold elastic cord:
    Cut into 3 pieces 5″ long.

Check your cupboards; you may have a glass or mug with a similar diameter that you could trace.

INSTRUCTIONS

Making the Base Cover

1. Place the 2 pieces of fusible interfacing end to end in the center of the wrong side of a piece of linen. Follow the manufacturer's instructions to fuse the interfacing in place.

2. Fold a piece of elastic in half to form a loop and pin to the short edge on the right side of the linen fabric. Repeat with the remaining 2 pieces of elastic. The first loop should be 1¹/₄″ from the top. The next loop should be 2¹/₄″ below the first loop. The last loop should be 2¹/₄″ below the second loop.

3. Stitch over the loops ¹/₈″ from the edge to tack them to the linen. Repeat if necessary to make sure the loops are secure.

4. With right sides together, sew the 2 pieces of linen along the top, the bottom, and the side with the loops. Clip corners, turn, and press.

5. Press under the raw edge ¼″ along the open side and pin. Topstitch ⅛″ from the edge to close.

6. To create a dart, lay the linen with the interfacing side down and pinch the fabric toward you, creating a small tucked fold along the top. Fold the fabric in half, bring it to the sewing machine, and sew ¼″ from the edge and 2¼″ deep, tapering the dart off the edge of the fabric as you sew. Sew the first dart approximately 3″ from the end with the button loops, and then add 6 or 7 more darts spaced approximately 3½″ apart along the top edge.

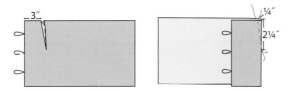

7. Wrap the linen cover around the stool and mark the placement of the buttons. Attach buttons with a needle and thread.

Upholstering the Stool Top

I. Lay the stool upside down on top of an end of the 14″ × 28″ foam, and trace around it with a pen or marker. Cut the foam along the circle using the serrated knife or scissors. Repeat to cut a second circle of foam.

2. Stack the 2 layers of foam onto the wooden stool and secure them with hot glue.

3. Trim the layers of foam into a dome shape using the serrated knife or scissors.

4. Lay the velvet fabric right side down on a work surface and place the stool upside down on the fabric. Pull the fabric over the foam and secure it to the underside of the stool with the staple gun. Then pull the fabric taut on the opposite side and staple in place. Continue working in opposite pairs of staples to secure the fabric, making sure the tension and gathers are evenly distributed around the circumference of the stool. Trim excess fabric.

5. Secure the white felt circles to the velvet top with glue.

French Macaron Mushrooms

These filled "mushroom" *macarons* are cute, unique, and not at all difficult to make. They produce a dessert that is as light and airy as the pixies who will nibble them up. We think you will love this recipe, but if you are short on time, you could decorate store-bought cookies with circles cut from fondant.

INGREDIENTS

Makes 15—20 double-layer macarons.

⅛ *teaspoon cream of tartar*

2 large egg whites

¼ *cup superfine baking sugar*

1 cup powdered sugar

¾ *cup almond meal/flour*

¼ *teaspoon purple gel food coloring*

Buttercream Icing (recipe on page 59) or your choice for filling

White fondant*

* Available at craft and baking supply stores; some types are premixed and precolored.

DIRECTIONS

You will need a baking sheet with a nonstick baking mat (such as Silpat) or parchment paper, assorted very small circle cookie cutters or fondant cutters, and a large plastic food storage bag with a corner cut off.

In a large bowl, add the cream of tartar to the egg whites. Whip with an electric mixer until soft peaks form. Sprinkle on the superfine baking sugar, and mix until you have stiff, glossy peaks. In a separate bowl, sift together the powdered sugar and almond meal/flour. Gradually fold together the flour-sugar mixture, food coloring, and egg whites. Once combined, with no white streaks, the mixture should be the consistency of thin toothpaste. Place it in the plastic bag, and pipe out circles about the size of a silver dollar onto the lined baking sheet. Leave at least 1˝ between dollops. Tap the baking sheet evenly on the counter 1—3 times to remove air bubbles and create smooth, even circles. Let the *macarons* rest 30 minutes before baking so they become less shiny and form a skin.

Preheat the oven to 375°F. Place the baking sheet in the oven and immediately reduce the temperature to 325°F. Bake for 10 minutes, rotating the tray at 5 minutes for even cooking. Let the *macarons* cool on the tray before removing them.

Sandwich the *macarons* in pairs with your choice of filling. On a smooth surface lightly covered with powdered sugar, roll out the fondant. Punch circles out of the fondant using the cookie cutters. Apply the circles to the *macarons* using a small dot of buttercream.

FOURTH OF JULY PICNIC

When our childhood summers began to stretch on just a little too long, the Fourth of July showed up just in time. Mom dressed us in our red, white, and blue, handed us pinwheels and outdoor toys, and shuffled us outside while she prepared fried chicken, corn on the cob, and Dad's favorite, cream cheese cherry pie.

Now, Mom and Dad have the day off to play with the grandchildren while we prepare the festivities. For this picnic party, we scooped all of the necessities into a basket and headed outdoors, making sure we had enough food to last an entire day of running through the sprinklers, playing Frisbee, and napping in the grass. Our checklist included stacks of classic white plates, baskets of flatware, and blankets for watching fireworks after the sun went down.

Summer, for us, is all about easy living, so every decoration had to be simple and functional. The fabric choices are inspired by the ruffle on a sundress and the cuff of a crisp, white summer shirt. We love that the runner and candle wraps work just as well for a Sunday picnic as they do for Independence Day. A Fourth of July banner pinned to the side of the burlap tablecloth gives a little extra patriotic flair.

Striped Table Runner

This striped table runner is patriotic yet versatile, giving a nod to the stars and stripes of the American flag without being quite so literal. A crisp, white ruffle ties in with the rest of the décor. We selected a heavy woven fabric that is hard wearing enough to stand up to years of picnics.

FINISHED SIZE:
18" wide × 104" long
(fits table 30" wide × 74" long)

Materials and Supplies

· White cotton fabric: 1⅓ yards for ruffle

· Navy-and-white striped woven fabric: 1¾ yards for runner

Cutting

White cotton fabric:

Cut 7 strips 6″ × width of fabric; sew strips together end to end.* From the joined strip, cut 2 strips 6″ × 148″.

Navy-and-white striped woven fabric:

Cut 3 strips, each 18″ wide × width of fabric. Sew strips together end to end* and then trim to 18″ × 105″.

Use the technique described in Clean-Finish Seam (page 154).

INSTRUCTIONS

1. Fold a 6″ × 148″ white strip in half lengthwise, right sides together, and sew the short ends using a ¼″ seam allowance. Turn right side out and press. Follow the instructions in Gathers and Ruffles (page 156) to create a gathered ruffle approximately 104″ long. Repeat with the remaining 6″ × 148″ white strip.

2. Fold a short end of the 18″ × 105″ striped fabric under ¼″ and press. Fold under ¼″ again, press, and topstitch. Repeat to hem other short end.

3. Pin the ruffle along the long side of the striped fabric with right sides together and raw edges aligned (Figure 1). Sew using a ½″ seam allowance. Trim the seam to ⅜″ wide, and overcast or zigzag the raw edges. Repeat to add the second ruffle to the other long side of the striped fabric.

4. Press each seam allowance toward the striped fabric, and topstitch the seam ⅛″ from the runner edge, using navy blue thread (Figure 2).

tip: *The runner can easily be adjusted for a shorter table. Simply measure the table's length and add 30″ to calculate the length of the woven fabric you will need. For the length of the ruffle strips, multiply the length of the runner by 1½ and then subtract 8″.*

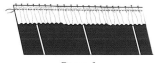

Figure 1

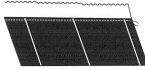

Figure 2

Ruffled Cuff Candle Wraps

For parties that stretch into the evening, few things are as charming as a picnic table aglow in candlelight. We dressed up plain glass candleholders with these wraps. Inspired by starched white cotton shirts, these candles have an easy, understated elegance that works just as well with paper plates as it does with fine china.

FINISHED SIZE:
Fits candleholder
measuring
3½" wide × 4" tall

Materials and Supplies

Makes 1 wrap.

- White cotton fabric: ¼ yard

- Buttons: 2 white or clear shirt buttons, ¾" (19mm) diameter

- Glass or plastic candleholder: 3½" wide × 4" tall

INSTRUCTIONS

I. Cut the following strips from white cotton fabric: 4" × 14", 4" × 12¾", and 2½" × 6½".

2. To create a placket for the buttons on the longest strip of fabric, turn a short side of the 4" × 14" strip under ¼" and press. Turn the fabric under again, this time 1", and press. Topstitch the placket in place along the first fold (Figure 1).

3. With right sides together and using a ¼" seam allowance, sew the placket and nonplacket pieces together along the top, the bottom, and a side edge. Do not sew the side with the placket. Turn right side out and press.

4. To prepare the ruffle, fold the 2½" × 6½" strip in half lengthwise, right sides together, and sew the short sides together using a ¼" seam allowance. Turn right side out. Baste the long open edges together using a ⅛" seam allowance. Pull the basting thread to gather until the ruffle is 3¼" long.

5. Sandwich the ruffle in the opening of the wrap. Distribute the gathers evenly, secure with pins, and topstitch, making sure the basting stitches are completely concealed (Figure 2).

6. Wrap the cuff around the candleholder, overlapping the end with the ruffle over the plain end, and pin. Remove from the candleholder and stitch the buttons in place, sewing through all layers of fabric. (The buttons are decorative, not functional.) Slide the wrap over the candleholder. If necessary, tack down the edges of the placket with a few hand stitches, sewing through the bottom layers of fabric only.

Figure 1

Figure 2

Fourth of July Garland

We love decorations that can be reused year after year, so we made this garland adjustable. Each of the fabric swags and medallions is a separate piece, attached to the tablecloth with safety pins. This way, it's easy to extend the table if you need more space. Prefer a more permanent solution? We have you covered—see the Tip (page 91).

FINISHED SIZE:
Each medallion
5″ diameter; each
fabric swag 22″ long
when draped

Materials and Supplies

Makes 1 garland as shown.

- Navy dot fabric: 1 yard for 3 medallions and 2 swags

- Assorted red, white, and blue prints: 3 squares 5″ × 5″ for medallion centers

- Batting: 5″ × 15″

- Flat wooden circles: 3¼″ diameter, 3 (available in craft supply stores)

- Pin backs: 1¼″ wide, 3 (available in craft supply stores)

- Hot glue

- Large safety pins (*optional*)

Cutting

The template pattern is on pullout page P1.

Navy dot fabric:
Cut 3 strips 4½″ × 16″ for medallion ruffles.
Cut 2 strips 8″ × 28″ for swags.

Assorted red, white, and blue prints:
Cut a 4½″ circle for each medallion, using the template pattern.

Batting:
Cut a 4″ circle for each medallion, using the dotted line on the template pattern.

INSTRUCTIONS

1. Using a hand-sewing needle, sew a long basting stitch around the edge of a fabric circle. Place a batting circle and a wooden circle in the center of the wrong side of the fabric circle, and pull the thread to cinch the fabric around the edges. Knot the thread to secure. Repeat to make 3 medallions.

2. Fold a 4½″ × 16″ ruffle strip in half lengthwise with wrong sides together, and baste the long, open edges using a ¼″ seam allowance. Pull the lower thread to gather and distribute the ruffle evenly around the medallion. Hand stitch it in place around the back edge of the medallion.

3. Attach a pin back to the back of the wooden circle with hot glue.

4. Hem each long edge of a swag piece using a narrow ¼″ rolled machine hem as described in Edge and Seam Finishes (page 154). Repeat with remaining swag pieces.

5. Baste along each short edge of each swag and pull the threads to gather to 2″. Topstitch the gathers to secure them.

6. Attach swags to the tablecloth using large safety pins. Cover with the medallions.

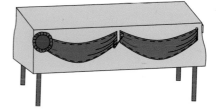

tip: *Would you prefer to have the garland all in one piece? Simply hand sew the basted edges of the garland swags to the backs of the medallions, sewing through the back layer of fabric only. In a hurry? Hot glue the basted fabric to the wooden circle instead.*

On a hot summer day, this cold, fluffy pie is what I looked forward to most. These days, it's my own children whom I have to keep from sneaking into the refrigerator before dinner for a taste. I am sure these super-easy pies will quickly become one of your family's favorites.

INGREDIENTS

Makes 2 pies, 9˝ each.

4 cups graham crackers

1 cup butter (2 sticks), melted

1 cup chopped pecans (optional—if you omit the pecans, add another cup of graham crackers)

8 oz. cream cheese, room temperature

2 cups powdered sugar

1 tablespoon milk

1 envelope of boxed whipped topping (Look for the boxed powder in the baking aisle at the grocery store. I used the Dream Whip brand.)

½ cup cold milk

1 teaspoon vanilla extract

2 cans cherry pie filling

DIRECTIONS

Preheat oven to 300°F. For the crust, crush the graham crackers and combine them with the melted butter and pecans. Pat the mixture into 2 pie pans, and bake for 10 minutes. Allow the crust to cool to the touch before starting the filling.

For the filling, thoroughly combine the cream cheese, powdered sugar, and 1 tablespoon milk with an electric mixer. Whip ½ cup cold milk with the vanilla extract and 1 envelope of boxed whipped topping. It will produce a light, fluffy whipped cream—like mixture. Add this to the cream cheese mixture, and combine thoroughly with a mixer. Divide the filling between the 2 pie pans. Spoon the cherry pie filling onto the pies. So simple, and you are done. Allow the pies to sit overnight in the refrigerator before cutting.

Photo by Jordan Söder

94

Handmade Hostess

LUAU PARTY

The idea of a luau may conjure up images of cheap grass skirt tablecloths, fake leis, and other party store decorations. While there is certainly nothing wrong with that, we had something more elegant in mind. We often daydream about tropical island getaways, so we wanted our guests to feel that they had been transported to a beautiful resort. Of course, living near the beach, as we do, helps. But even if you are totally landlocked, these projects will help you make over your yard into a place dripping with Hawaiian-inspired luxury. Our luau tablecloth, made in rich, shimmery fabrics in a range of greens, is decidedly upscale. Fresh

flowers and ti leaves can really elevate the look of the party. To create layers of texture and interest, we placed felt flower napkin rings and an oversized fabric hibiscus alongside real orchids. No orchids? Look for flowers with bold colors and graphic shapes, or use a sculptural potted plant.

The table is decorated with a few seashells and our handmade coconut candles. The crowning glory is the cake itself, covered in toasted coconut, and pretty enough to be a centerpiece all on its own. By the time the sun goes down, we think your guests will be feeling utterly indulged.

Luau Tablecloth

The luau tablecloth is made from individually sewn leaves in four shades of green fabric. The range of tones gives the tablecloth depth. Our version fits a standard folding table 24″ × 48″ with leaves covering three sides of the table, but this project can easily be adapted to any size or shape. To measure and cut the table top and back pieces for your own table, see Measuring (page 98).

FINISHED SIZE:
Fits table
24″ wide × 48″ long × 28½″ high

Materials and Supplies

- Interfacing: 9 yards lightweight fusible interfacing (20″ wide), such as Pellon 911FF Fusible Featherweight

- Green sateen fabric: 10½ yards total in a range of tones (We used 2¾ yards each of forest green and grass green, 2 yards of moss green, and 1½ yards each of lime green and chartreuse.)

- Natural linen: 1½ yards for top

- Green linen: 2¼ yards for back side of table

tip: *For other projects, such as Fabric Flowers (page 52), using the right interfacing can make or break a project. These leaves are more forgiving, so grab something on sale. Here are a few other budget-conscious ideas:*

- *Use inexpensive fabric for the reverse side of the leaves and cut the yardage requirements for the green fabric in half.*

- *Instead of using a cotton/silk blend fabric, try dyeing muslin several shades of green.*

- *Make the leaves from poster board or heavy paper. Use the template pattern provided and staple to the top piece of fabric.*

Cutting

The template patterns are on pullout page P2. Enlarge 200%.

Fusible interfacing:
   Cut 13 large leaves and 12 small leaves from fusible interfacing using the template patterns.

Natural linen:
   Cut 1 piece 25″ × 49″.

Green linen:
   Cut 1 piece 29½″ × 74″.

INSTRUCTIONS

1. Fuse 13 large fusible interfacing leaves to 3 shades of green fabric (5 forest, 5 grass, 3 moss), leaving at least 1″ between fusible interfacing shapes. Fuse 12 small interfacing leaves to 2 shades of green fabric (6 lime, 6 chartreuse), leaving at least 1″ between fusible interfacing shapes.

2. Lay the fabric with the fused leaves face down on a second layer of fabric, pin, and cut around each leaf shape, leaving a rough ½″ seam allowance. (If you prefer, cut fabric and interfacing separately and then fuse, as you would a standard pattern.)

3. With right sides together, stitch around the outline of each leaf directly on the edge of the interfacing, leaving the base of the leaf open. When you reach the point of the leaf, shorten the stitch length to 1.5mm. Trim seams to ¼″, clip corners, and turn.

Shorten the stitch length near the point.

4. Press the leaf with a hot iron beginning at the pointed end and working toward the base of the leaf. Topstitch down the center of the leaf.

5. Hem the bottom and side edges of the green linen for the back of the tablecloth using a ¼″ rolled machine hem (page 154). Follow the instructions in Gathers and Ruffles (page 156) to gather the upper edge of the fabric.

6. Place the natural linen fabric on the table with the wrong side facing up. Pin the smaller leaves to the right side, along the edge, by lifting the edge of the linen. Then add the larger leaves, wrapping a leaf at a 90° angle around each corner. Pin the gathered green linen panel to the back edge of the tablecloth.

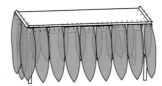

7. Baste the leaves and linen to the tabletop fabric using a ½" seam allowance. Turn the tablecloth right side out and check placement of the leaves. Stitch, using the basting stitches as a guide.

8. Trim the seams to ⅜" and overcast the edges with a 3-step zigzag, if your machine has it, or a regular zigzag. Turn and press.

MEASURING

To create a different-sized tablecloth, measure the top of the table. If you have a lightweight folding table, you can lay the fabric flat on the floor and turn the table upside down over it. Trace the tabletop directly on the fabric with tailor's chalk and add in seam allowances. For a rectangular or square table, add 1" to each of the length and width measurements. For a round table, add a ½" seam allowance around the circumference of the circle.

The fabric for the back of the table is measured as follows: the width of the table multiplied by 1.75 × the height of the table, plus 1" for seam allowances. If the table can be viewed from all angles, omit this step and consider making additional leaves to cover the back as well as the front and sides.

Hibiscus Napkin Rings

The felt hibiscus flowers lend a pop of color to the table. These beautiful napkin rings look challenging, but you'll get a great result if you start with nice, crisp shapes. Be sure to check Sewing Felt (page 155) for tips.

FINISHED SIZE:
Flowers are 3″ wide.

Materials and Supplies

Makes 1 flower.

- Fuchsia felt: 8″ × 8″

- Gold felt: 2″ × 3″

- Green felt: 4″ × 4″

- Narrow green velvet ribbon: 1 yard

- Small rubber band or hair elastic

- Fabric glue

- Hot glue gun

Cutting

The template patterns are on pullout page P1. Enlarge 200%.

Fuchsia felt:
    Cut 5 petals.

Gold felt:
    Cut 1 of each stamen piece.

Green felt:
    Cut 2 leaves.

Velvet ribbon:
    Cut 1 piece 4″ long.
    Cut 1 piece 26″ long.

INSTRUCTIONS

1. Use fabric glue to secure the 2 yellow stamen pieces together so they form a stamen.

2. Use hot glue to attach the 2 leaves to each other at *both* pointed ends, leaving an opening in the center where the ribbon tie will pass through.

3. Gather the ends of the 5 petals in your hand, a petal at a time, fanning them out and arranging them into a hibiscus shape (Figures 1 and 2). Refer to Fabric Flowers (page 53) to see how this technique was used to create the large roses. Insert the stamen into the center of the flower. Wrap the bottom of the petals securely with a rubber band.

4. Hold an end of the leaves in place next to the base of the petals. Wrap the 4″ piece of velvet ribbon around the base to cover the elastic band (Figure 3) and secure in place with hot glue.

5. Slide the 26″ ribbon through the opening in the leaves and tie it around the napkin. Trim ends of the ribbon at an angle.

Figure 1

Figure 2

Figure 3

Large Hibiscus Flower

The oversized hibiscus flower (shown in the lower right photo on page 94) uses the same technique as the oversized roses in Fabric Flowers (page 52). Enlarge the large hibiscus petal and stamen template patterns 200% (pullout page P1), and follow the rose instructions, except that you will add a stamen as you did for Hibiscus Napkin Rings. We made our large hibiscus flower using cotton sateen for the petals and yellow cotton for the stamen.

Coconut Candle

You can purchase similar candles, but we had fun making these ourselves. We love the earthy, natural look of these coconut candles, which are still slightly fuzzy, unlike their party store counterparts. Cutting your own coconut comes with a sweet reward. As with any candle, be sure to keep flames supervised.

FINISHED SIZE:
3" × 5"

Materials and Supplies

Candle supplies are available at craft supply stores.

- Coconut
- Hammer
- Nail
- Sharp knife

- Melt-and-pour candle wax
- Prewaxed wick
- Vanilla candle fragrance

CANDLE INSTRUCTIONS

1. Hammer a nail into the coconut (or use an electric drill) to make a small hole; drain the milk. Wrap the coconut with a towel, and hit it with a hammer near the hole to crack it in half.

2. To hollow out the coconut, use a sharp knife to score the flesh in a checkerboard pattern. Use a spoon to pop the coconut meat out.

3. Melt clear wax in an old steel pot on the stove, following the manufacturer's instructions. Add a small amount of vanilla fragrance.

4. Cut the wick to 5" long. Hold the wick carefully as you pour the wax into the hollowed-out coconut shell. Hold the wick in place for a few minutes until the wax sets.

5. Once the wax cools the first time, it will leave an indentation around the wick. Pour more wax into the top. Trim the wick with scissors to ½" long before lighting.

REBECCA'S RECIPE:

Coconut Cake

It is always a delight to bake something that looks as yummy on the outside as it tastes on the inside. This coconut cake is an adaptation of my mother's Italian cream cake recipe. Straightforward and simple to make, it creates a delicious and beautiful dessert. Here, the toasted coconut will get everyone into that island mood.

INGREDIENTS

2 cups sugar

½ cup shortening

½ cup butter (1 stick)

5 eggs

2 cups flour

1 teaspoon baking soda

1 cup buttermilk

1 teaspoon vanilla extract

16 oz. shredded coconut for batter and decoration

Cream Cheese Icing (recipe follows):

   2 packages (8 oz. each) cream cheese

   1 cup butter (2 sticks), at room temperature

   32 oz. powdered sugar

   2 teaspoons vanilla extract

DIRECTIONS

You will need 2 buttered and floured 8˝ round cake pans.

Using an electric mixer, combine the sugar, shortening, and butter until light and fluffy. Add the eggs and mix well. In a separate bowl, whisk together the flour and baking soda. In a third bowl, mix the buttermilk and vanilla extract. Alternate adding the flour mixture and the buttermilk mixture to the butter mixture. Stir in 1 cup of the coconut. Divide the batter equally into the 2 pans. Bake at 350°F for 25 minutes, or until a toothpick comes out clean. Do not overbake. Let the cakes cool completely before icing.

Place the bottom cake layer on a plate and spread icing on the bottom layer. Place the second layer on top and repeat. Insert 3 wooden skewers in a triangular pattern so the cake will not shift while you finish icing it.

Place the remaining coconut in a pan on medium to high heat, stirring constantly. When it starts to turn light brown, transfer it immediately to a plate. Apply a smooth layer of icing around the entire cake, including the top. Gently press toasted coconut around the sides. Decorate the top with flowers if you wish. Refrigerate cake, and then allow to come to room temperature before serving.

CREAM CHEESE ICING   Cream together the **cream cheese**, 2 sticks **butter, powdered sugar,** and 2 teaspoons **vanilla extract.**

Handmade Hostess

MAD SCIENTIST PARTY

Birthday parties for boys tend to be very lively, so we decided to capture all of that manic energy and channel it right into our theme. Our birthday guest of honor became a mad scientist for the day, complete with blue hair, plenty of mad scientist laughter, and his very own lab coat.

We set up activity stations with a goo glob beanbag toss, science experiments, and "eyeball" birthday cupcakes with a special gooey surprise inside. Everything is safe to play with, including the pet rat stuffie, plastic beakers with cotton smoke, and labware full of bouncy eyeballs, syringes, and colored-water "chemicals."

If you're bracing for a team of mad scientists at your home, plan ahead for messes. Spills don't need to spoil the fun as long as they are in designated areas and you have plenty of paper towels on hand.

Trading off activity stations with another adult can be a great way to preserve your energy and let others get in on the fun, too. You might be surprised at how enthusiastic some of the other adults will be at playing mad scientist for the day. In fact, we think this is a fun decorating theme whether your guest of honor is turning 5 or 50.

Goo Globs

No mad scientist party would be complete without some experiments. These "slime" beanbags and wall decorations are experiments that Mom won't object to; they require no cleanup. Attach the wall globs anywhere—to clothing, windows, and tablecloths. The beanbags are perfect for a no-holds-barred game of beanbag toss.

FINISHED SIZE:
4½"–6¼" across for beanbags and 9"–13" across for wall decorations

Materials and Supplies

• Lime green felt: ½ yard

• Orange felt: ½ yard

• Electric blue felt: ½ yard

• Dry black beans: approximately ½ cup for each glob

tip: A single sheet of 8½" × 11" acrylic felt is enough to make a large felt goo glob beanbag. However, we recommend purchasing ½ yard of each color and using the leftover fabric for wall and table decorations.

INSTRUCTIONS

The template patterns are on pullout page P2. You can enlarge them 200% or print them in a variety of different sizes as you prefer, or even cut them freehand.

1. For the beanbags, cut 2 beanbag pieces out of each color—green, orange, and blue. Use the felt cutting techniques described in Sewing Felt (page 155).

2. Using a ⅜″ seam allowance, sew around the edge of the 2 beanbag pieces, leaving a 2″ opening.

3. Fill the beanbag with at least ½ cup of dry beans and no more than ¾ cup, and stitch the opening closed.

4. For the wall decorations, simply cut out single shapes in assorted sizes and colors.

5. Stick the shapes to the wall using double-stick tape or painter's tape. (Test in an inconspicuous spot on the wall to make sure it is safe for the wall paint.) Goo globs can also be taped to clothing, windows, and tablecloths.

Pet Rat

This sweet little pet rat was the star of the party, eating up gummy worms and climbing all over the table as if he owned the place. We think you will find this soft, squishy rat to be just the right size to fit in small hands and pockets.

FINISHED SIZE:
4½" tall

Materials and Supplies

- Gray fabric with nap: ¼ yard soft fabric, not too thick (such as faux suede or velveteen)

- Cream corduroy fabric: 4" × 8" for feet, paws, and tail

- Pink cotton fabric: 2" × 3" for ears

- Black beads: 2 for eyes, 5mm*

- Pink embroidery floss: for nose

- Polyfill stuffing

- Chopstick or other turning tool

* Substitute black embroidery floss to make the eyes, instead of beads, if this project is intended for a small child.

Cutting

The template patterns are on pullout page P2.

Gray fabric:

Cut 1 head.

Cut 1 body front.

Cut 1 bottom.

Cut 2 body backs
(1 and 1 reversed).

Cut 2 arms.

Cut 2 ears.

Cut 2 forearms.

White corduroy:

Cut 2 paws.

Cut 4 feet.

Cut 1 strip 1" × 4"
for the tail.

Pink fabric:

Cut 2 ears.

INSTRUCTIONS

All seams are ⅜" unless otherwise indicated.

1. With right sides together, sew the straight edge of a paw to the short end of a forearm. Lay the assembled piece right sides together with an arm piece, and hand stitch around the arm, leaving the short, straight end open (Figure 1). Turn right side out. Insert stuffing with the end of a chopstick. Repeat for the other arm.

2. Place 2 foot pieces right sides together, and stitch around the curve. Turn right side out and stuff. Repeat for the other foot.

3. With right sides together, stitch a pink ear to a gray ear, leaving the straight edge open. Turn right side out. Repeat for the other ear.

4. Fold the corduroy tail strip in half lengthwise with right sides together. Stitch along the length and across a short side. Clip corners and turn the tail right side out. If the fabric is too thick to turn, you can also roll a strip of fabric into a tail shape and whipstitch closed.

5. Stitch 2 darts in the head piece, as indicated on the template pattern. Roll the head piece into a cone shape with the right side of the fabric facing in, and stitch the side of the cone closed (Figure 2).

6. With right sides together, sew the 2 body back pieces together along the long straight edge.

7. With right sides together, align the front and back body side seams and pin in place. Insert the arm into this seam about two-thirds of the way from the bottom edge, and pin, making sure that the white paw is facing the front. Sew the side seam, stitching through all layers of the arm. Repeat for the other side, making sure that the arms are the same length and in the same position on the body (Figure 3).

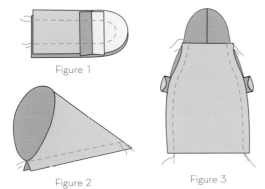

Figure 1

Figure 2

Figure 3

8. The body of the rat should now be a tube. With right sides together, pin the top half of the head to the body back. Pinch each ear in half and insert into the seam with the pink side facing the head, pinning as you did with the arms. Stitch around the top half of the head from side seam to side seam (Figure 4). Pin the bottom half (the "chin") to the body front, and sew from side seam to side seam.

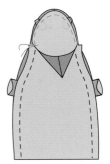

Figure 4

tip: *When sewing on ears and feet, it helps to turn the piece right side out and check the positioning before you sew. Details such as how long you make the arms, or the angle of the ears, will lend your rat his or her own special personality.*

9. With right sides together, pin the bottom piece to the lower edge of the body front, inserting the feet. Stitch from side seam to side seam through all layers of fabric. Turn the rat right side out and stuff.

10. Using a blind hem stitch (page 154), close the gap around the back side of the rat, inserting the tail as you stitch.

II. Embroider the rat's nose with 2 strands of pink embroidery floss, using a satin stitch and burying the thread tails.

12. Using a knotless start (see Hand Sewing, page 155), attach the 2 black beads for the eyes of the rat. To make a rat that is safe for small children, omit the black beads and use a satin stitch with black embroidery floss to embroider the eyes instead. Bury the thread tails as you finish.

Every mad scientist needs a lab coat, and while this one looks impressive, it's actually quite simple. The "coat" is really an apron, with only four pattern pieces. Since the coat ties on, it should last through a few growth spurts. To create an ID badge for each guest, use prepared cards as described below, and photograph guests as they arrive.

FINISHED SIZE: Boys' size 5–6

Materials and Supplies

- White cotton: 1½ yards

- Interfacing: ¾ yard lightweight interfacing (20″ wide), such as Pellon 911FF Fusible Featherweight

- White bias tape: double-fold, ½″ wide, 2 yards

- Buttons: 3 clear or white shirt buttons, ½″ diameter

- White card stock: for the badge

- Camera and photo printer: for the badge

- Plastic badge holder (available at office supply stores or online)

Department of Experimental Medicine

Dr. Kaden
Brain Surgeon

Mad Scientist Lab Coat and Badge

summer

Cutting

The template patterns for the lab coat and badge are on pullout page P2. Enlarge lab coat pieces 200%.

White cotton:

 Cut 4 lab coat front pieces (2 and 2 reversed).

 Cut 1 pocket.

 Cut 2 collars.

 Cut 2 front facings (1 and 1 reversed).

Lightweight fusible interfacing:

 Cut 2 front facings (1 and 1 reversed).

 Cut 1 collar.

Figure 1

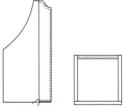

Figure 2 Figure 3

Base of collar

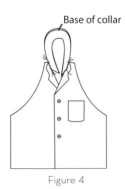

Figure 4

INSTRUCTIONS

Lab Coat

1. Fuse the interfacing to the facings and a collar piece, following the manufacturer's instructions.

2. Place the collar pieces right sides together and stitch around the outside of the collar, leaving a 3″ opening along the bottom edge (Figure 1). Clip corners, turn the collar right side out, and press.

3. With right sides together, using a ¼″ seam allowance, sew a front piece and a reversed front piece together along the shortest side edge. Turn right side out and press. Repeat with remaining 2 front pieces.

4. With right sides together, sew a facing to the front pieces, stitching from the bottom edge up and across the top of the facing (Figure 2). Clip corners, turn the facing right side out, and press. Repeat for the opposite side.

5. Refer to Edge and Seam Finishes (page 154) to hem the bottom of the coat using a rolled machine hem.

6. Turn under the top edge of the pocket ⅛″, turn again ¼″, press, and topstitch. Turn under the sides and bottom of the pocket ⅛″ and press (Figure 3). Pin the pocket to the front of the lab coat as indicated on the template pattern and topstitch in place along the sides and bottom.

7. Lay the front pieces right side up and overlap them. Attach shirt buttons to the front of the lab coat, stitching through all layers of fabric. (The buttons are decorative, not functional.)

8. Fold down the top edge of the facing to create the collar's lapel, and press.

9. With right sides together, place the base (the shorter of the 2 long sides) of the collar on the folded edge at the top of either lapel. Pin in place, and stitch to attach collar to each lapel (Figure 4).

Handmade Hostess

10. Find the midpoint of the bias tape. Place the base of the collar inside the bias tape fold. Pin the bias tape to the collar and underarm seams of the lab coat. Sew along the length of the bias tape, encasing the front and collar (Figure 5).

11. Press the collar and tack it down with a few hidden stitches (Figure 6).

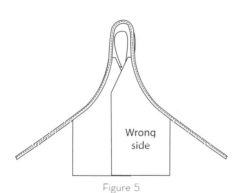

Figure 5

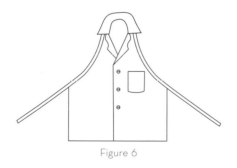

Figure 6

Scientist Badge

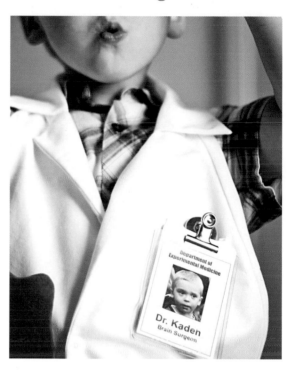

With a Polaroid camera or a digital camera and small photo printer, you can create a custom scientist badge for each child as guests arrive at the party. Before the party, print out the scientist credentials (pullout page P2) on white card stock, and cut out a window for the picture. Personalize each badge with a guest's name. Do a test run before the party using a photo of your child, so you know how to take and print a photo the correct size.

As the guests arrive, shoot a photo of each child and print it out. (Consider putting another adult or teen in charge of this process.) Tape the photo in place behind the card stock, and then slide both into a purchased plastic badge holder.

Mad Scientist Cupcakes

This fun dessert was inspired by my mental picture of a mad scientist in his dark laboratory, his hair sticking up in all directions, surrounded by jars filled with goo, worms, syringes, and eyeballs. What kid doesn't love biting into an eyeball cupcake and pulling out a worm? This treat will bring lots of smiles from your guests.

INGREDIENTS

Makes 24 cupcakes.

Cupcakes

2 cups sugar

1¾ cups all-purpose flour

¾ cup high-quality cocoa powder

1 teaspoon salt

1½ teaspoons baking powder

1½ teaspoons baking soda

2 eggs

½ cup vegetable oil

1 cup milk

2½ teaspoons vanilla extract

1 cup boiling water

Cupcake pan and liners

Toothpicks

Decorations

White, colored, and black fondant*

Powdered sugar (for rolling fondant)

3 circle cookie or fondant cutters in ½˝, 1½˝, and 2¼˝ sizes

1 bag of gummy worms

Buttercream Icing (recipe on page 59)

* Available at craft and baking supply stores; some types come premixed and precolored.

DIRECTIONS

Preheat oven to 350°F. Stir together the first 6 dry ingredients until well incorporated. Add the eggs, oil, milk, and vanilla extract; whisk together until smooth, or beat with an electric mixer on medium/high speed for a couple of minutes. Slowly stir in boiling water. Carefully pour the thin batter into the lined cupcake pan, filling each cup half full. Bake 22 to 30 minutes, or until a toothpick inserted in the cakes comes out clean. Allow to cool completely before frosting.

On a smooth surface lightly covered with powdered sugar, roll out the white fondant less than ¼˝ thick using a rolling pin coated with powdered sugar. Cut circles with a circle cookie cutter or biscuit cutter the size of the cupcakes. With a slightly smaller cutter, repeat the process with the colored fondant to create the iris of each eye. Repeat using a very small circle with the black fondant to create the eye pupil. Once the fondant circles are dry, stack them on top of each other to create an eye, using a dab of water to make them stick together.

Poke a hole through the top of each cooled cupcake, and push a gummy worm inside. Spread Buttercream Icing on top of the cupcake. Place the fondant eyeball on top of the icing and push gently so it lies flat on the cupcake.

EXTRA TOUCHES

To make the Mad Hatter hats, use brown felt and refer to the Leprechaun Hat Place Card Holders instructions (page 42) and template pattern (pullout page P1). Attach red ribbon sashes and card stock tags with hot glue. A template pattern for the Mad Hatter's 10/6 tag is on pullout page P1.

The mini topiaries came from the wedding aisle of the craft store. We hot-glued tiny red and white roses to them.

For the green "grass" place mats, simply cut out squares or other shapes from pieces of Astroturf, available from your local building supply store.

116

MAD HATTER'S TEA PARTY

We were always on the hunt for white rabbits and secret doors to Wonderland, so for this party it seemed vitally important to make the entryway as magical as the party itself. We spent an afternoon creating this fanciful archway (and attracted quite a few curious neighbors in the process).

On the other side of the arch waited a table worthy of the Queen of Hearts herself, with whimsical teapots, miniature Mad Hatter hats, and a fabric topiary decorated with red roses. To complete the table, we layered green artificial grass place mats on top of a bright red tablecloth.

To re-create this look, use white ramekins, teacups, cake plates, and dishes; supplement your own with thrift store finds. To maximize visual appeal, stack items of varying heights and shapes, and group them in arrangements of three or five. We used adhesive putty to hold the dish stacks in place. Still, we didn't use anything we couldn't bear to have broken or chipped—especially outdoors.

After tea, our guests enjoyed a game of croquet using funny flamingo mallets and fancy croquet hoops. Rebecca served up delicious crème brûlée in teacups—much more fun than boring old bowls.

The best part of a Mad Hatter's Tea Party is surprising guests with something a little unexpected. We hope you enjoy your own adventure down the rabbit hole just as much as we did.

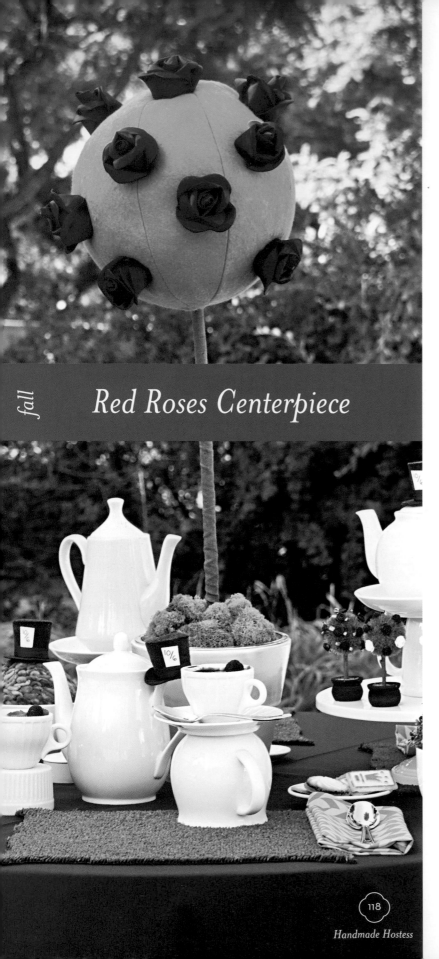

fall

Red Roses Centerpiece

You don't always have the luxury of throwing a party in the center of a rose garden, so why not create the garden yourself? This whimsical centerpiece is sewn from felt and decorated with fabric roses, which are miniature versions of the ones found in Fabric Flowers, page 52. The roses are pinned rather than stitched in place, making them easier to arrange and rearrange.

FINISHED SIZE: 10½" across × 34½" tall

Materials

Makes 1 topiary with 9 roses on the front side only.

- **Green felt:** ¾ yard for topiary sphere

- **Red sateen fabric:** 1¾ yards for roses*

- **Brown fabric:** ⅛ yard for stem

- **Interfacing:** ¾ yard fusible interfacing (44" wide), such as Pellon Decor-Bond*

- **Polystyrene foam balls:** 1 each, 10" ball and 6" ball

- **Dowel:** ⅝" wide × 26" tall

- **Sturdy pot or vase:** at least 6" across the top

- **Floral moss**

- **Dressmaker pins:** extra-long, nickel-plated steel

- **Batting**

* If topiary will also be viewed from behind, double the yardage for the interfacing and red fabric.

Cutting

The template patterns are on pullout page P1. Enlarge 200%.

Green felt:

Cut 8 topiary sphere pieces.

Brown fabric:

Cut 1 strip 2½″ × 15¾″.

Fusible interfacing:

Cut 36 outer petals and 9 inner petals.

INSTRUCTIONS

Making the Topiary

1. Place 2 topiary sphere pieces right sides together. Stitch along a side using a short stitch length and a ¼″ seam allowance. Repeat with remaining sphere pieces to create a total of 4 pairs.

2. Sew pairs together until all 8 pieces are attached in a long strip.

3. Bring the free edges together and sew the top 3″ closed. Backstitch to secure.

4. Trim seam allowances to ⅛″, and turn the fabric right side out. Wrap the 10″ polystyrene foam ball in batting, and slide the topiary cover over it. Arrange batting to get a nice, round shape.

5. Using a hand-sewing needle and thread, refer to Hand Stitches (page 154) to slipstitch the back side of the topiary closed, leaving a ¾″ opening at the bottom for the dowel.

6. Fold the brown fabric in half lengthwise and sew along the long edge with a ¼″ seam allowance. Turn right side out.

7. Press the dowel 6″ into the bottom of the topiary sphere through the opening in the felt cover. With a hand-sewing needle and thread, sew a running stitch around the opening in the topiary sphere felt, cinch closed, and knot.

8. Slide the brown fabric cover from Step 6 over the free end of the dowel until it meets the sphere. Hand stitch it to the bottom of the topiary.

9. Place the 6″ foam ball into the pot. Insert the free end of the dowel approximately 4″ into the foam ball. Cover the top of the pot with moss.

tip: If the base is too wobbly, secure the foam ball inside the pot with hot glue.

Creating the Roses

1. Follow the manufacturer's instructions to fuse all (outer and inner) rose petal fusible pieces to the wrong side of the red sateen, leaving at least ½″ between fusible pieces. Lay the fabric with the fused petals right sides together with a second layer of red sateen, pin, and cut around the petals, leaving a rough ¼″ seam allowance. The interfacing will be the sewing guide, so the seam allowance does not need to be exact.

2. Stitch around each petal directly on the edge of the interfacing, using a short stitch length. Leave a 2″ gap along the bottom. Clip curves and the V shape of the petal, and turn.

3. Press fabric under ¼″ along opening, and topstitch to close. Repeat to make a total of 36 outer petals.

4. Sew 2 inner petals right sides together, leaving a 2″ gap along the bottom edge. Clip corners and turn. Press fabric under ¼″ along the opening, and topstitch to close. Repeat to make 9 inner petals.

5. Starting with the pointed end, roll the inner petal around your finger or a pencil to create a tight spiral (Figure 1). Use a dress-maker pin to secure the rose center directly to the topiary (Figure 2).

6. With your fingers, shape each outer petal into a curve. Pin each of the 4 outer petals in place, working in opposites from the center to the outer edge (Figures 3 and 4). Hide the pins on the inside of each petal. Angling the pins will help to create the shape.

7. Fold down the upper edge of the rose petals after you have pinned them in place (Figure 5).

Figure 1

tip: *Like tying a bow, it can take some practice to get a nice-looking rose. If you have trouble on your first try, don't give up! The petals are very forgiving and can be easier to work with the more you have handled them. If the rose begins to look too rumpled, simply iron the petals and start again.*

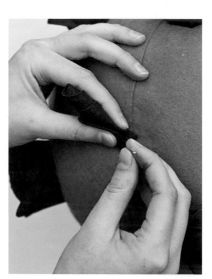

Figure 2

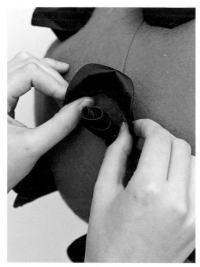

Figure 3

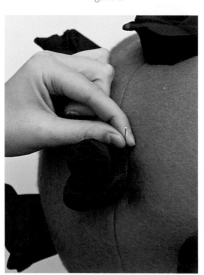

Figure 4

Figure 5

Handmade Hostess

It only takes a little imagination and some paint to transform a regular old croquet mallet into something as silly and improbable as a flamingo. The hoops are miniatures of the Welcome to Wonderland Archway (page 123).

Finished size:

7″ wide × 25½″ tall (1 mallet)

Materials and Supplies

- **Wooden croquet set and hoops** (look in thrift stores for a used set)

- **Sandpaper**

- **Painter's tape** (*optional*)

- **Acrylic paint:** red, white, black, yellow, and purple

- **Clear sealant:** such as Mod Podge or polyurethane

- **Googly eyes** (available in craft supply stores)

- **Garland of artificial greenery** (available in craft supply stores)

- **Heart-shaped ornaments:** nonbreakable

- **Fishing line**

- **Hot glue gun**

Queen's Croquet Set

fall

INSTRUCTIONS

1. Lightly sand the wooden croquet mallets to remove any old paint or sealant. Wipe with a damp paper towel to remove dust.

2. For Steps 2–4, use painter's tape to tape off a section at a time, referring to the photo (page 121) for placement guidance. Let paint dry before removing tape and adding the next color. Apply 2 coats of yellow paint to the nose of the mallet to create a "beak."

3. Paint the mallet head and lower half of the handle red or purple for the body.

4. Paint the top half of the handle white. After the paint has dried, wrap tape around the handle to create stripes placed 1" apart, and paint with 2 coats of black paint. Remove tape and touch up any areas where needed. Let dry.

5. Apply sealant to entire mallet and let dry.

6. Adhere googly eyes to either side of the mallet head using hot glue.

7. Clean and prepare the croquet balls as you did the mallets, and paint them with 2 coats of black paint. Decorate balls with white polka dots or stripes. Apply 2 coats of sealant.

8. For the hoops (photos on pages 116 and 121), cut strips of garland the length of a hoop, and wrap them around the metal frame.

9. Tie the garland securely to the frame in at least 3 places (the center and either side) using fishing line.

10. Attach a plastic, nonbreakable ornament to the center of each hoop with fishing line.

Handmade Hostess

This freestanding, portable archway is a showstopper that will have neighborhood children lining up to see it. The PVC pipe base just slips over rebar in the ground.

FINISHED SIZE: Approximately 3' wide × 4'10" tall

Materials and Supplies

Most of these supplies can be found at a hardware or building supply store.

- PVC pipe: 1½" wide, 18' piece

- PVC pipe connectors: 1½" diameter, 45° bend, 6

- Hula hoops: 2

- PVC pipe cutter (if needed; see Tip, page 124)

- Green spray paint

- Duct tape

- Garland or pine roping: We used artificial "long-needle pine" swags from a craft supply shop.*

- Moss ribbon: 3" wide, 12' long (available at craft stores)

- Miniature teacups

- Heart-shaped ornaments: nonbreakable

- Fishing line

- Rebar: 2 pieces 3' long

- Rubber mallet

* The amount needed varies with the fullness of the garland. We used 30 fairly thin 1-yard swags.

Welcome to Wonderland Archway

fall

INSTRUCTIONS

I. Using a PVC pipe cutter, cut 6 pieces of 1½" PVC pipe 3' long. Attach a 45° bend connector to an end of each piece.

tip: *Many hardware stores will cut the PVC pipe for you. If this is not an option, a cutter specially designed to cut through PVC pipe is inexpensive. We selected a thin 1½" pipe that would be easy to cut.*

2. Gather 3 pipes together and wrap securely with duct tape. Repeat for the remaining 3 pipes. These are the sides of the arch.

3. Cut the hula hoops in half with scissors. Insert the hula hoop ends into the pipe connectors, and secure with duct tape. Tape the other end of each hula hoop into the opposite side. Repeat until all pipes have a hula-hoop arch in place.

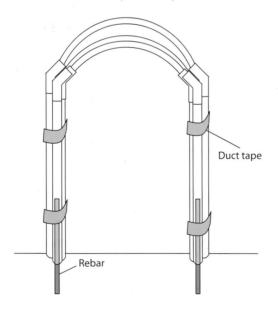

Duct tape

Rebar

4. Spray paint the PVC pipe and the hula hoops green.

tip: *The arch will be flimsy until it has been inserted over the rebar supports. To decorate it, consider working outdoors. Pound the rebar into the ground with a rubber mallet so that the rebar sticks out of the ground by approximately 2'. (We promise this sounds harder than it is.) Slide the arch over the rebar supports.*

5. Beginning at the top left side, drape the garland over the top of the archway. The garland should almost stay in place by itself as you work, but you may need a second pair of hands in some places. Cut lengths of fishing line and tie around the garland to secure it.

6. Continue tying on lengths of garland on either side, arranging it to look as full as possible from the front.

7. Wrap moss ribbon around either side of the arch for decoration.

8. Tie small teacups and heart-shaped ornaments onto the arch with fishing line.

tip: *If you are transporting a finished arch to a park or other location, bring extra garland and fishing line with you to make any touch-ups or last-minute repairs.*

Rebecca's Recipe:

Teacup Crème Brûlée

I love collecting tea sets and am always looking for an excuse to use them. Here we used teacups to serve one of my favorite desserts, crème brûlée. This beginner-friendly recipe produces a dessert with the trademark hard, sugary exterior, but it requires no cooking, giving you more time to get ready for your special guests.

INGREDIENTS

Makes about 10 teacupfuls.

2 packages (3.5 oz. each) instant vanilla pudding

2 cups heavy cream

1 cup milk

2 teaspoons vanilla extract

Granulated sugar

Raspberries for garnish

Mint leaves for garnish

DIRECTIONS

You will need a propane torch. If you don't have one, you can put the desserts under a broiler for 2–3 minutes maximum, but keep the oven door open and watch very carefully.

Combine the first 4 ingredients using an electric mixer with a whisk attachment at high speed. Beat until fluffy and thick. Place the mixture in a large plastic bag, and let it chill in the refrigerator for an hour.

Cut a corner off the plastic bag and use it to pipe the filling into the teacups. Smooth out the top of the filling with a spoon dipped in warm water. Apply a thick, even layer of sugar on top, and brown the sugar with a propane torch. Keep the torch moving the whole time to brown the sugar evenly.

Garnish each dessert with a raspberry and a mint leaf.

EXTRA TOUCH

To create the chandelier, we wrapped two wire hoops of different sizes in black ribbon and tied them together using silver cord. For easier hanging, cut all of the silver cord into even lengths and hot glue the knots to the hoops so you get a symmetrical shape. To create the bats, tape the bat body and both bat wing template patterns (pullout page P2) together to form a single pattern. Do not enlarge the patterns. Cut two of the bat shapes from felt. Stitch ⅛" around the edge, leaving a 2" opening. Stuff the bat with polyfill and then topstitch to close the opening. Suspend three bats and five orange ornaments from the hoops to complete the haunting effect.

HALLOWEEN BASH

The best haunted houses of our childhood were homegrown affairs thrown by adults who knew how to get in on the fun. For our party, we designed projects that we would enjoy reusing from year to year. With these, any space—living room, backyard, or garage—can be transformed into a place for pirates and witches to mingle.

After disguising the living room with a fabric backdrop, we decided to glam things up with some ruffles and shiny fabric. The Witch's Skirt Tablecloth is the perfect spot to display treats. We turned our backs for just a minute, and it looks like our chair was turned into a witch—or was it the other way around? These funny stuffed legs and witch's boots will make any chair a conversation piece.

We wanted to dress up the room with an elegant chandelier, but ours was taken over by bats! These felt creatures spent the evening hovering over the table and eyeing the "monster" cupcakes. And oh—what cupcakes they were! We are fans of easy but unique desserts on a night when you already have so much else going on. Rebecca explains how you can make quick work of these festive cupcakes and be ready to join in on the fun.

Witch's Legs Chair

Children and adults alike will get a laugh over this funny chair. Make one as the focal point of your party or sew up a bunch for a matching set.

FINISHED SIZE: Fits standard dining room chair; finished leg approximately 14½" tall

tip: This project works best with a chair that does not have stretchers between the legs. However, you can adapt it by hand-sewing the legs closed around the cross bars. First, measure the height and circumference of the chair's legs. If the legs are more than 14½" tall and 15" around (after adding polyfill), then you will need to adapt the fabric measurements in Cutting (next page).

Materials and Supplies

Yardages are based on 44"-wide fabric unless otherwise noted.

- Orange sateen fabric: ⅝ yard

- Black cotton fabric: 2 yards

- Black felt: 36" wide, ¾ yard

- Cardboard or heavy card stock: 4" × 6" for buckles

- Orange glitter

- Polyfill stuffing

- Hot glue gun

Cutting

The template patterns are on pullout page P2. Enlarge 200%.

Orange fabric:

Cut 14 strips 1½″ × 15″ for the legs.

Cut 4 strips 1¾″ × width of fabric for the chair pad ruffle.

Black fabric:

Cut 14 strips 1½″ × 15″ for the legs.

Cut 2 strips 1¾″ × width of fabric for the chair pad ruffle.

Cut 4 strips 3½″ wide × 22½″ long for the ties.

Black felt:

Cut 4 (2 and 2 reversed) witch's shoe pieces using the template pattern.

Cut 2 pieces 4″ × 10½″ for the shoe collars.

Cardboard:

Cut 2 buckles using the template pattern.

INSTRUCTIONS

This chair has 2 separate witch's "legs" and a ruffled tie-on witch's "skirt" seat cover.

Making the Legs

1. Sew 14 of the 1½″ × 15″ strips together, alternating orange and black, to create a piece of striped fabric measuring 14½″ × 15″. Fold the striped fabric in half, right sides together, and sew along the 15″ edge using a ¼″ seam allowance. Turn the fabric right side out. Repeat with remaining 1½″ × 15″ orange and black strips.

2. Slide the fabric tubes over the front chair legs. Hand sew around the top of each leg with a running stitch, cinch closed, and knot the thread.

3. Stuff the legs firmly with polyfill from the bottom openings. Fluff the stuffing with your hands first, pulling it apart into small pieces. Use a chopstick or similar object to get a firm shape.

4. Sew each pair of shoe pieces right sides together (Figure 1). Clip the curves, and turn. Pin a shoe collar to the top of the outside of a shoe, overlapping the shoe more in the back than the front (Figure 2). Hand stitch the collar to the shoe along the inside edge, and fold to the outside. Repeat with remaining shoe and shoe collar.

5. Slip the shoes onto the ends of the chair legs. Take a few stitches to tack the back of each shoe to a striped leg, so they won't slip off when the chair is moved.

6. Decorate the cardboard shoe buckles with glitter, and adhere them to the shoes using hot glue.

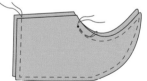
Figure 1

Figure 2

Making the Seat Cover

1. Sew 2 orange 1¾″ × 44″ strips together end to end. Join remaining 2 orange strips in a similar fashion. Repeat with 2 black 1¾″ × 44″ strips. Hem the long edge of a joined orange strip, using a ¼″ rolled machine hem as described in Edge and Seam Finishes (page 154).

2. Sew the long strips together to make an alternating 3-piece stripe of orange, black, and orange (Figure 3). Hem the short ends of the pieced strip. Make a cut across the pieced strip approximately 22″ from an end. This short piece is for the back of the chair. Hem the ends where you just cut. Gather each strip as described in Gathers and Ruffles (page 156), and set aside.

3. Chair seats are generally not flat, straight surfaces, so draping is the best way to get a custom fit for the seat cover. Drape the black fabric (or a piece of muslin to practice) over the chair seat. Decide how long an overhang you will need to cover up the top of the witch's legs, keeping in mind that you will be attaching a 3½″ ruffle around the edge. With tailor's chalk, mark the edges of the chair on the fabric.

4. Cut out the fabric along the markings, and cut out a second, identical piece for the cover's underside.

5. Place the top piece back on the chair, and pin the corners in place (Figure 4). Mark notches where the chair's back is attached. Cut along the markings. Repeat on the bottom piece.

6. With right sides together, sew the front corners on the top piece, and trim the extra fabric (Figure 5). Repeat for the bottom.

7. Fold a black 3½″ × 22″ strip in half lengthwise with right sides together, and stitch along the long edge and a short side using a ¼″ seam allowance. Clip corners, turn, and press. Repeat with remaining 3 strips.

8. Place the long ruffle and 4 ties in place along the outer edge of the right side of the seat front (Figure 6). Place the seat back on top of the front piece with right sides together. Adjust the ruffles to fit, pin, and stitch around front sides and notches, using a ¼″ seam allowance (Figure 7). Leave the back edge of the cover open. Clip corners, turn, and press.

9. Press the raw edges of the fabric under ¼″ along the back edge. Insert the raw edge of the short ruffle into the opening, adjust to fit, and pin in place. Topstitch across the opening.

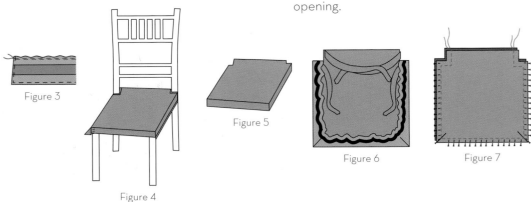

Figure 3

Figure 4

Figure 5

Figure 6

Figure 7

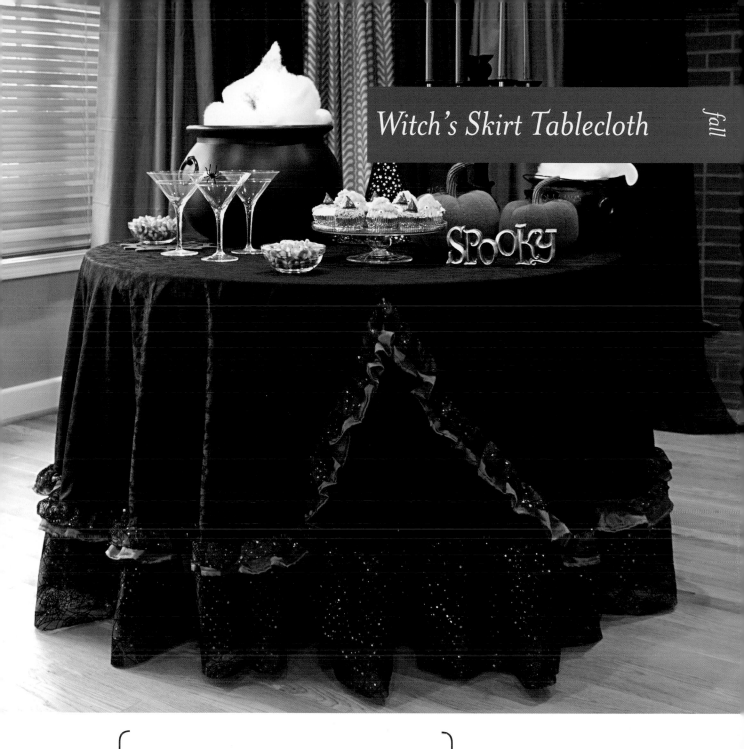

Witch's Skirt Tablecloth

This tablecloth features 45 yards of ruffles, so be sure to check out our ruffle-sewing tips in Gathers and Ruffles (page 156). However, we think all of that gathering is worth it! The end result is dramatic and surprisingly glamorous.

FINISHED SIZE:
108" diameter (fits table 48" diameter × 28½" high)

tip: *If your table is a different size from ours, refer to the chart in Round Tables (page 157) to figure out the tablecloth's finished diameter.*

Materials and Supplies

Yardages are based on fabric with a usable width of at least 44".

- Black brocade: 5 yards for tablecloth*

- Spider web lace novelty fabric: 5½ yards for ruffles

- Orange sateen fabric: 1¾ yards for ruffle

- Tailor's chalk

- Heavy string: 50"

* If the black brocade fabric has less than a 44" usable width, you will need more fabric.

Cutting

Black fabric:

Cut 2 pieces 90" × width of fabric for the top.

Novelty spider web fabric:

Cut 3 strips 3" × 180" for the ruffles.

Cut 3 strips 11" × 180" for the ruffles.

Orange sateen:

Cut 9 strips 4" × 60" for the ruffles.

tip: *The instructions here conserve fabric by creating a ruffle that is hemmed on one edge. However, it is faster to create a folded ruffle. Simply double the width of the strips, and fold them in half before gathering. Save even more time by selecting a novelty fabric that does not fray, and leave the edge unfinished.*

INSTRUCTIONS

To make the ruffles for this tablecloth, refer to Gathers and Ruffles (page 156).

I. Sew the 2 black 90″ × width of fabric pieces together along the longest edge, using a ½″ seam allowance, to create a single large piece. Use the instructions in Clean-Finish Seam (page 154) for a nice finish.

2. Referring to Drafting a Large Circle (page 157) for guidance, adjust the string so it measures 42½″ between the center point and the tailor's chalk. Draw the circle and cut out the tablecloth.

3. Sew the 3″-wide novelty fabric strips end to end into a piece 15 yards long. Trim the ends as shown (Figure 1). Hem the long curved edge using a ¼″ rolled machine hem (page 154). Gather the strip into a ruffle.

4. Repeat Step 3 with the 4″-wide strips of orange fabric.

5. Repeat Step 3 with the 11″-wide novelty fabric strips, but do not curve the ends.

6. Drape the round black tablecloth on the table, and mark a point with tailor's chalk at the edge of the table where the tops of the ruffles will meet to create a swag effect. Position the 3″-wide novelty ruffle as shown (Figure 2). (Right sides should be facing, so the ruffle will be upside down.) Distribute the ruffles evenly, and pin. Stitch in place using a ⅜″ seam allowance. Repeat to add the orange ruffle on top of the novelty ruffle. If the ruffles do not lie flat, press and then topstitch along the ruffles ⅛″ from the seam.

7. Pin the 11″-wide novelty ruffle around the base of the tablecloth (Figure 3), overlapping the ends by ½″ on the back side. This time do not follow the swag, but instead pin the ruffle around the outer circumference of the circle and stitch using a ⅜″ seam allowance. Trim, and then finish the seam allowance with a 3-step zigzag if your machine has it, or a regular zigzag, if desired. Topstitch in place, if necessary.

Figure 1

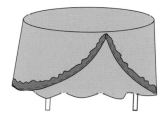

Figure 2

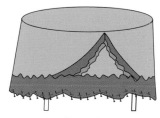

Figure 3

Sleepy Bat

Photo by Jordan Söder

FINISHED SIZE: 11½″ × 16″

This sleepy stuffed bat has soft wings sewn in black velvet. We used pipe cleaners to give the top edge of each wing a rigid shape.

Materials and Supplies

Makes 1 bat.

- Black velvet or velveteen: ⅓ yard

- Black sateen: ¼ yard

- Black felt: 4″ × 4″

- Pipe cleaners: 2

- Polyfill stuffing or wool batting

- Freezer paper

- Fabric glue

- Embroidery floss: white and orange, for face

Cutting

The template patterns are on pullout page P2. Enlarge the bat body, wing, and leg template patterns by 200%. Do not enlarge the bat claw template pattern.

Black velvet:

Cut 4 wings (2 and 2 reversed).

Cut 4 legs (2 and 2 reversed).

Black sateen:

Cut 2 body pieces.

Freezer paper:

Cut using the dashed lines on the enlarged template patterns.

Cut 2 wings (1 and 1 reversed).

Cut 1 body.

Cut 2 legs (1 and 1 reversed).

Black felt:

Cut 6 claws using template pattern, or cut freehand.

Photo by Jordan Söder

INSTRUCTIONS

1. Fuse the freezer paper to the wrong side of the wings (1 and 1 reversed), the legs (1 and 1 reversed), and the body.

2. Place the 2 bat wings right sides together, and stitch around the outside edge using the freezer paper as a guide. Remove freezer paper, clip corners, and turn.

3. Sew a channel ½" from the top edge of the bat wing (Figure 1). Stuff the lower portion of the wing firmly with polyfill.

4. Fold an end of a pipe cleaner under ¼" and insert it into the channel of the wing.

5. Repeat Steps 2–4 for the other wing.

6. Place 2 bat body pieces right sides together, and stitch around the outside edge using the freezer paper as a guide. Leave openings as marked for the wings and legs (Figure 2). Clip curves, and turn right side out.

Figure 1   Figure 2

7. Sew 2 legs right sides together. Remove freezer paper, clip curves, and turn. Repeat for the other leg. Stuff the legs firmly with polyfill, and attach felt claws with fabric glue or a few hand stitches.

8. Stuff the bat body with polyfill. Insert the legs and wings into the body of the bat, and stitch closed (by hand or machine) through all the layers.

9. Embroider eyes, nose, and mouth using white and orange embroidery floss. Alternately, you can glue on face details from felt, just like the bat claws.

For Halloween, I like cupcake decorating ideas that are unique yet easy to make. I chose purple icing "hair" for Tootsie Roll—hatted witch cupcakes, and neon green for googly-eyed monsters. (You will need a piping bag and various tips to achieve these effects.) We offer a yellow cake recipe here; to make chocolate cupcakes, use the recipe for Mad Scientist Cupcakes (page 114). You can use the Buttercream Icing from the Petit Fours (page 59). Of course, you may use a cake mix and ready-made icing instead. We'll never tell!

INGREDIENTS

Makes 24 cupcakes.

1 cup unsalted butter (2 sticks), at room temperature

2 cups granulated sugar

2 teaspoons vanilla extract

4 large eggs, at room temperature

4 cups plus 2 tablespoons cake flour (not self-rising)

1½ teaspoons baking soda

2 teaspoons baking powder

1 teaspoon salt

2 cups buttermilk (You can substitute 2 cups whole milk with 2 tablespoons vinegar added; let sit for 5 minutes.)

For the witch cupcakes:
Icing in purple and black
Miniature Tootsie Rolls

For the monster cupcakes:
Miniature marshmallows
Icing in neon green, white, and black
Candy eyeballs (available in the baking aisle at most grocery stores)

DIRECTIONS

You will need a cupcake pan and liners, and a piping bag and various piping tips.

Preheat oven to 350°F. Cream the butter and sugar with an electric mixer until pale and fluffy. Add the vanilla extract and eggs. Sift 1 cup of flour with baking soda, baking powder, and salt, and add to the batter. Alternate adding the buttermilk and remaining flour. Beat until well incorporated; *do not overmix.* Fill the lined cupcake pan three-fourths full.

Bake for 22–30 minutes, checking cupcakes after 22 minutes. They are done when a toothpick inserted in the top comes out clean. Let them cool before frosting.

WITCH   Use a piping bag and a tip #233, which has many small holes in it, to cover the top of the cupcake with purple frosting "strands of hair." Microwave a miniature-size Tootsie Roll for 10 seconds on high. Roll it out on waxed paper and use a small, circular cookie cutter to make the brim of the hat. Microwave a second Tootsie Roll, and make a cone shape. Gently apply this to the brim. Using a very small piping tip (#1 or #2), pipe a black line of frosting in the crevice between the top of the hat and the brim. Place the hat on the cupcake.

MONSTER   For the green monster, use icing as glue to stack marshmallows into a mound shape on top of the cupcake. Place the neon green frosting in a piping bag. Using a piping tip #12, squeeze out the frosting, allowing it to slide down the mound in ripples. Repeat around the entire cupcake until you get a green glob. Gently press the candy eyeballs into the frosting. For the other monster, pipe on white icing as shown in the photo (previous page) and add eyeballs.

Handmade Hostess

THANKSGIVING GATHERING

For most of our childhood, we lived thousands of miles away from our extended family. While we enjoyed our fair share of traditional Thanksgivings with Mom's home cooking, we also branched out, dining with other families to see how they celebrated. That's not to say that we don't have our own special traditions. Every Thanksgiving involved some discussion of what we were thankful for, and we always came home to the smell of freshly baked pumpkin pie and pecan tarts.

Now that we are hosting our own Thanksgivings, we hope to keep that spirit of fun and the unexpected alive in our celebrations. For this gathering, the *Mayflower* replica sailing above the table captures the daring and wonder of the Pilgrims' brave voyage while still leaving plenty of room for the dishes. Small felt launch ships float on tulle-and-cardboard waves, serving as the centerpiece and the perfect vehicle for writing a grateful message to each guest. On each plate a napkin sports a simple, gleaming fall decoration.

Thanksgiving is a wonderful time to savor the very best that fall has to offer—apple cider, turkey, mashed potatoes, and boundless blessings. By the time your Thanksgiving meal is complete, you'll be ready to curl up and dream of all the holiday magic that is yet to come.

Mayflower *Ship*

This Mayflower replica is fashioned out of shimmering metallic fabrics and would look equally grand hung over a buffet table or an entrance. Although not difficult to make, this project can be time consuming. But you can use this special decoration year after year; the sails are decorative, not structural, so you can remove the dowels for easy fold-up storage.

FINISHED SIZE: 19″ × 21″

Materials and Supplies

- Gold sateen, taffeta, or other silky fabric:* 44″ wide, 1 yard for ship's exterior

- Lining fabric:* 44″ wide, 1 yard for ship's interior

- White cotton fabric: ½ yard for sails

- Interfacing:
  1 yard heavy-duty interfacing (20″ wide), such as Pellon Peltex 70 Ultra-Firm Stabilizer

  1 yard lightweight fusible interfacing (20″ wide), such as Pellon 911FF Fusible Featherweight

materials and supplies continued

Cutting

The template patterns are on pullout page P2. Enlarge 200%.

materials and supplies continued

- **White nylon twist cord:** 1/8" wide, 2 1/2 yards to gather lower sails

- **Thin gold or white nylon cord:** 6 yards for rigging

- **Gold bias tape:** 1/2" wide, 1 2/3 yards

- **Cotton cord:** 1/4" wide, 1 2/3 yards for piping

- **Gold ribbon:** 1/4" wide, 1 1/2 yards to connect jump rings

- **Jump rings:** 3/8" (10mm) diameter, 22

- **Wooden dowel:** 3/16" diameter, 36" long

- **Craft knife or rotary cutter:** to cut dowel

- **Zipper foot for sewing machine**

- **Bodkin**

- **Gold tulle:** 1 yard (*optional*)

* Refer to Sewing Silky Fabrics (page 155).

Gold fabric:
    Cut 2 side panels (1 and 1 reversed).*
    Cut 1 back piece.*

Lining fabric:
    Cut 2 side panels (1 and 1 reversed).*
    Cut 1 back piece.*

White cotton fabric:
    Cut 2 upper sails.
    Cut 2 squares 7 1/2" × 7 1/2" for lower sails.
    Cut 1 triangle sail on the fold.

Lightweight fusible interfacing:
    Cut 2 sides (1 and 1 reversed).
    Cut 1 back.

Heavy-duty interfacing:
    Cut 2 side panels (1 and 1 reversed) using dashed lines on the template pattern.
    Cut 1 back piece using dashed lines on the template pattern.

Gold ribbon:
    Cut 7 pieces, each 3" long.
    Cut 15 pieces, each 1 1/2" long.

Nylon twist cord:
    Cut 8 pieces, each 10" long.

Wooden dowel:
    Cut 2 pieces 4 3/4" for the upper sails.
    Cut 2 pieces 6 1/2" for the lower sails.
    Cut 1 piece 5 1/2" to hold rigging.

* Place pattern pieces on the bias.

INSTRUCTIONS

Making the Ship Body

I. Center a heavy-duty interfacing side piece on the wrong side of a fabric side panel. Repeat for other side.

2. Fuse a lightweight interfacing side piece to the wrong side of each piece from Step 1.

3. Create a plank pattern by sewing horizontal parallel lines of stitching approximately ⅝″ apart on each side panel. The ship's back panel is left plain.

4. Place the heavy-duty fusible interfacing on the wrong side of the ship's back panel. Layer the lightweight interfacing back piece on top of the heavy-duty interfacing and fuse in place.

tip: *Sew the lining first. This will give you a chance to practice piecing the curves in the ship's stern.*

5. With right sides together, sew the ship's lining side panels together from the front of the ship to the back, leaving a 4″ opening along the bottom. End seam at dot and backstitch.

6. With right sides together, stitch the back lining in place between the 2 side lining pieces, easing in curves (Figure 1). Stop at the dot and backstitch. Set lining aside.

7. With right sides together, assemble the fabric sides and back as with the lining in Steps 5 and 6, but do not leave an opening along the bottom. Turn fabric ship right side out.

8. To create piping, wrap the bias tape around a piece of cotton cording with right side facing out. Using a zipper foot, baste ¼″ from the open edge of the bias tape (Figure 2).

9. Starting at the back of the ship, pin the piping to the outside of the ship along the top edge. Overlap the ends.

10. Machine baste the piping in place, stitching as close to the piping as possible (Figure 3).

11. Insert the ship exterior piece (right sides facing out) inside the lining (wrong sides facing out). Loop a 3″ piece of ribbon through a jump ring. Repeat to create a total of 7. Pin a ribbon loop upside down between the exterior and lining at the 4 top corners, at the center back, and midway along each side. Refer to the project photo (page 140) for guidance in placing the ribbon loops. Stitch all around the top of the ship (see Tip, page 143). Trim corners.

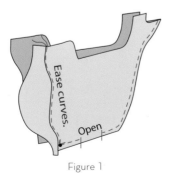

Figure 1

Figure 2

Figure 3

tip: *If you flip the piece inside out so that you are looking at the wrong side of the ship's exterior fabric, you can use the previous stitches as a guide. Stitch around the top between the basting stitches and the stitch line you created when you sewed the piping to the exterior pieces.*

12. Flip the piece right side out by pulling the exterior fabric through the opening in the lining. Fold the raw edges of the opening under ¼" and topstitch the folds together to close the opening. Push the lining into the ship exterior. Topstitch around the top of the ship, if desired.

Sewing the Sails

1. Turn an edge of a 7½" × 7½" lower sail under ¼" and press. Turn fabric under ¼" again and press for a rolled machine hem. Topstitch the hem. Repeat with remaining lower sail.

2. With the hem from Step 1 at the bottom, create a channel by pressing a side under ¼". Fold again ½" from the first folded edge and press. Stitch as close to the inner folded edge of the channel as possible.

Sew another seam, dividing the channel into 2 even channels. Repeat this step on the other side of the sail (Figure 4).

3. Repeat Step 2 with remaining lower sail.

4. Use a bodkin to feed a 10" length of ⅛"-wide nylon twist cord into each of the channels. Fold the raw top edge of the sail under ¼" and topstitch, catching the cords in the seam. Fold this stitched edge over a 6½" dowel and pin in place. Wrap a 1½" ribbon around a jump ring, insert on a side of the sail within the folds created for the dowel, and pin in place. Repeat on the other side. Remove the dowel and machine stitch along the dowel pocket, catching the ribbon loops (Figure 5). Pull the cords to gather the sail slightly on either side, and tie in a bow (see project photo, page 140). Repeat this step with remaining lower sail.

5. For the upper sail, create a ¼" rolled machine hem on either side as described in Edge and Seam Finishes (page 154). Fold the bottom edge under ¼" twice, and press. Sandwich 2 of the 1½"-long ribbon loops with jump rings on either corner. Stitch in place (Figure 6). Repeat this step with remaining upper sail.

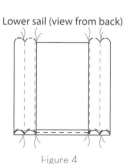

Lower sail (view from back)

Figure 4

Figure 5

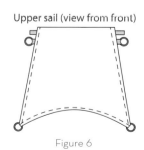

Upper sail (view from front)

Figure 6

6. Turn the top edge of an upper sail under ¼" and press. Fold this edge around the wooden dowel and pin in place. Remove the dowel. Insert 1½" loops of ribbon with jump rings on either side of the sail within the folds created for the dowel, and secure with pins. Stitch along the first fold, catching the ribbon loops, to create the dowel pocket. Repeat with remaining upper sail.

7. For the triangle sail, fold the bottom edge under ¼", creating a miter at the point. Fold under ¼" again and topstitch. Fold the sail in half, right sides together, and pin a ribbon loop with jump ring near the top. Stitch the vertical straight edge, catching the ribbon loop (Figure 7).

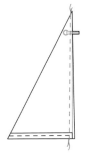

Figure 7

8. Turn the sail right side out, and sandwich a ribbon loop with jump ring in either lower corner, as shown (Figure 8). Topstitch to close the opening.

9. Insert dowels in the pockets at the top of each lower and upper sail. Thread the rigging cord through the ribbon loops and jump rings, using the photo (page 140) as a guide. Begin by tying the 5½" dowel from something such as a closet rod. The 5½" dowel acts as a spacer for suspending the sails. First add the top and bottom sails in the center of the ship, then add the top and bottom sails in the front, and finish with the back sail. Leave the cords long until all sails are threaded. Once the ship is threaded and balanced, cut notches in the 5½" dowel to keep the cords in place, and tie tightly to secure.

Figure 8

10. Fill the ship with tulle, if desired.

fall

These frothy ocean waves of tulle and cardboard leave plenty of room on the table for dishes and can be easily moved aside if you need more room for the turkey. For the tulle, one long line of basting stitches up the center is all you need. (After sewing the Mayflower, all good Pilgrims deserve a break!)

FINISHED SIZE:
3" wide × 57" long × 7½" high

Materials and Supplies

- **Gold tulle:** 1 yard

- **Gold ribbon:** ¼″ wide,
  13 yards

- **Large cardboard boxes:** 2

- **Gold card stock:**
  21 pieces, 12″ × 12″

- **Ruler and craft knife**

- **Hot glue gun**

- **Gluestick**

INSTRUCTIONS

You will need 2 rows of cardboard waves; the tulle is placed between them to cover the inner cardboard support.

Cardboard Waves

The template patterns are on pullout page P2. Enlarge 200%.

1. To make a support for the waves, cut a cardboard box into strips 12 wide. Tape enough strips together to create a piece 12″ × 57″. Using a ruler and craft knife, score the cardboard lengthwise at 3″, 6″, and 9″ (Figure 1).

tip: *Cardboard density varies, but generally speaking, score the cardboard once on each side to fold or twice on each side to cut.*

2. Fold the cardboard along the score marks and tape it into a long, narrow box shape.

3. Wrap the cardboard box support with gold card stock.

4. Using the template patterns, cut out 12 large waves and 4 double waves from a cardboard box. Arrange cardboard waves on either side of the long, narrow box from Step 3 and make small marks on the long box showing placement of each wave (Figure 2).

tip: *If you plan to display the wave centerpiece on a buffet table or other surface where the back side will not be visible, you can cut your work in half by covering only one side of each wave with gold card stock.*

Figure 1	Figure 2

5. Using the cardboard waves as templates, trace the large wave 24 times (12 and 12 reversed) onto the gold card stock. Trace 2 large waves on each 12″ × 12″ piece of card stock by placing the template as shown (Figure 3). Trace the double wave 8 times (4 and 4 reversed) onto the gold card stock. Cut out the shapes. Using a gluestick, attach the gold card stock to the front and back of each wave.

6. With hot glue, apply narrow gold ribbon along the top exposed edge of each wave to hide the cardboard.

7. Using hot glue, affix the waves along each side of the long box (Figure 4).

Tulle Center

1. Cut the tulle into 3 strips 12″ × width of fabric. Piece together end to end to get a strip 12″ × approximately 120″, and sew with a long basting stitch down the center of the strip. If you don't want to join the strips together, you can simply feed each strip of tulle through the machine end to end. No seams are necessary since the tulle will not fray, and any gaps will be concealed in the gathers.

2. Gather the tulle, and tie the thread ends securely. Place the tulle between the front and back waves.

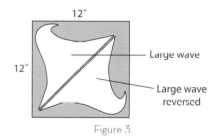

Figure 3

Figure 4

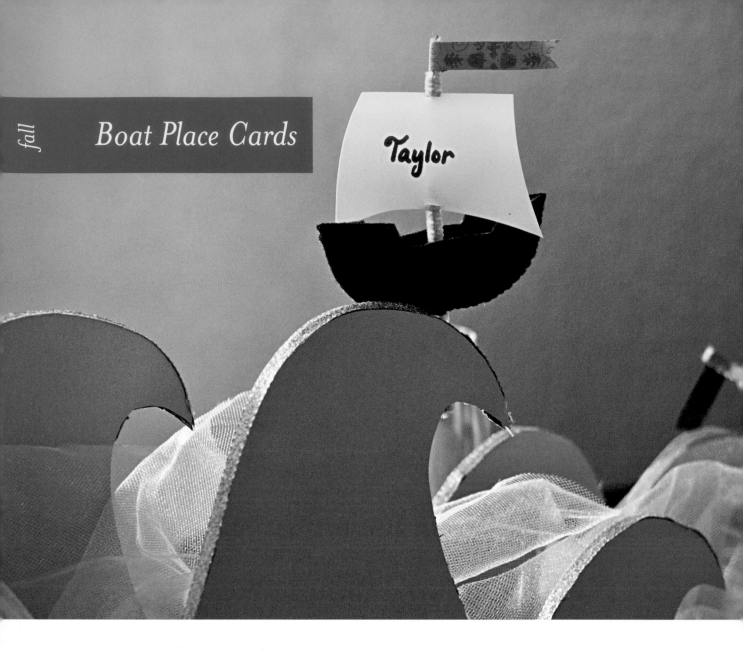

FINISHED SIZE: 3¾" wide × 4" tall

Your guests will be enchanted to find their very own boats sailing on soft tulle waves. The pipe cleaner mast does double duty as a hidden stand on the back side of the boat. If you wish, tuck a personal message or Thanksgiving blessing inside each boat. Inside Taylor's boat is a favorite Thanksgiving quote: "We can only be said to be alive in those moments when our hearts are conscious of our treasures." —Thornton Wilder

Materials and Supplies

Makes 1 boat.

- Brown felt: 4″ × 4″ for boat base

- Orange paper: 1″ × 3″ for flag

- Beige pipe cleaner: 1

- White card stock: 3″ × 4″ for sail

INSTRUCTIONS

The template patterns are on pullout page P2.

I. Cut 2 boat base pieces from the brown felt. Place the pieces together and, following the instructions in Sewing Felt (page 155), top-stitch along the curved bottom of the boat. When you have reached the center of the curved bottom, take a single extra-long stitch. This opening will leave room to insert a pipe cleaner.

2. Cut out a sail from the white card stock and a flag from the orange paper. Write a guest name or message on the sail (see Tip below).

tip: *Don't like your handwriting? You can use a computer to print out your guests' names in a font of your choice and trace those letters onto the white sail with a gold pen.*

3. Cut 2 small slits on the sail using scissors or a craft knife where noted on the template pattern. Thread the pipe cleaner through the base of the boat, leaving a 1″ tail under the boat. Form the tail of the pipe cleaner into a circle and bend it so the circle is horizontal. The circle will serve as a base for the boat to rest on. Thread the rest of the pipe cleaner through the slits in the sail. Fold the end of the paper flag around the pipe cleaner, and glue in place. Trim any excess pipe cleaner.

tip: *For an extra-fun touch, use pipe cleaners in autumn colors to make silly finger puppets that will entertain younger guests while you wait for everyone to arrive. See examples in the lower right photo on page 138.*

Add color and sparkle to your place settings with some brown felt and inexpensive glass ball ornaments. A length of ribbon and an autumn leaf complete this simple but elegant napkin ring.

FINISHED SIZE: Acorns approximately 1" diameter

Materials and Supplies

Makes 1 napkin ring.

- Brown felt: 2″ × 3¾″ for acorn caps

- Glass ball ornaments: 1⅛″, in autumn colors, 2

- Artificial autumn leaf: 1

- Ribbon: ¼″ wide, 12″ piece

INSTRUCTIONS

I. Cut a piece of brown felt 1″ × 3¾″.

2. Referring to Sewing Felt (page 155), sew the short ends of the brown felt together using a ⅛″ seam allowance to create a cylinder. Make sure that the top half of a glass ball ornament fits comfortably inside the cylinder.

3. Using long stitches, baste along the top edge of the felt cylinder. Cinch the threads to gather, leaving a ¼″ opening for the ornament hanger, and knot the threads.

4. Roll the unfinished edge of the felt cap ⅛″ to the outside, and hand sew in place. This will create a nice round acorn cap shape.

5. Insert the ornament in the cap so the hanging loop protrudes from the top.

6. Repeat Steps 1–5 to make another acorn.

7. Thread the 2 acorns onto the ribbon. Wrap ribbon around napkin and tie in the back. Poke the leaf stem through a hanging loop to keep it in place.

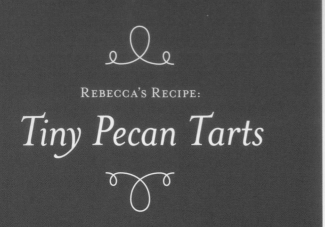

REBECCA'S RECIPE:

Tiny Pecan Tarts

I will never be able to eat a pecan tart without thinking of Mom and her well-loved tart pan, along with the old tin containers she stored the pecan tarts in—or rather, the tins that I would sneak pecan tarts out of. The heavenly smell of sugar and pecans would beckon us downstairs so that by the time the tarts were ready, we were already hanging out in the kitchen. I dare you to try eating just one.

INGREDIENTS

Makes 3½ dozen.

8 oz. cream cheese

1⅓ cups plus 2 tablespoons butter, softened

2⅔ cups flour

2 eggs

1½ cups brown sugar

2 teaspoons vanilla extract

Dash of salt

1⅓ cups pecans, broken into pieces

DIRECTIONS

You will need mini tart pans.

FOR THE PASTRY   Mix together the cream cheese, 1⅓ cups butter, and flour. Press the dough gently into tart pans.

FOR THE FILLING   Mix together the eggs, brown sugar, 2 tablespoons softened butter, vanilla extract, salt, and pecans. Preheat the oven to 325°F. Fill each tart two-thirds full. Bake for 25 minutes.

SPECIAL
TECHNIQUES

Edge and Seam Finishes

Unless otherwise noted, fabric should be sewn right sides together with a ¼″ seam allowance.

Rolled machine hem   The basic rolled machine hem in the book requires pressing and folding the fabric under by ¼″ and then turning under another ¼″ and pressing. Topstitch close to the edge of the first fold.

Clean-finish seam   Sew a ½″ seam and press it open. Fold each side of the seam under ¼″ and press. Topstitch each seam allowance, stitching only the seam allowance, to create a neatly finished seam.

Hand Stitches

Backstitch

French knot

Satin stitch

Blanket stitch

Chain stitch

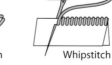

Whipstitch

Slip stitch

Blind hem stitch

Sewing Felt

Felt is a wonderful and forgiving material to work with, but a few tricks can make the difference between a mediocre project and a masterpiece. Where possible, try to purchase felt with the highest wool content you can afford; 100% wool felt can be expensive, but it produces beautiful, long-lasting results. In many of the projects in this book, we used a widely available wool/rayon blend felt by National Nonwovens (see Resources, page 158). A wool/rayon blend is a great compromise between quality and price for the types of projects in this book. Inexpensive acrylic felt, such as the kind found in craft stores, tears and stretches easily, so stitches have a tendency to pull apart and shapes will not be as crisp.

Cutting

The secret of a beautifully sewn felt item begins with proper cutting techniques. We highly recommend using freezer paper, found in most grocery stores. Freezer paper is like waxed paper with the wax on only one side.

1. Trace the template pattern onto the dull side of the freezer paper.

2. Leaving a wide margin around the shape, cut out the freezer-paper template and press it with an iron, shiny side down, onto the felt, to temporarily adhere it. Always test your iron on a scrap piece of felt first to make sure it will not melt.

3. Cut through both the felt and the freezer paper, using the traced shape as a guide for a crisp, precise shape. Peel off the freezer paper.

Hand Sewing

Two basic stitches are used in the felt projects in this book: the whipstitch and the blanket stitch (see page 154). We recommend an embroidery needle and embroidery floss. We always use a knotless start. Cut a length of embroidery floss 36" long and separate out a single strand. Fold the embroidery floss in half and thread both tails through the eye of the needle. Insert the needle through the fabric and stop before the loop at the end goes all the way through. Take a tiny backstitch, slipping the needle through the looped end. Now you are ready to begin sewing.

Sewing Silky Fabrics

If you are planning to use a slippery fabric (especially an inexpensive one such as acetate taffeta), keep in mind the following tips.

- Cut the fabric on the bias. For a small project, the cost difference is quite minimal, and many fabrics cooperate better this way.

- Take care with ironing. Some shiny fabrics may not iron well, which may pose a problem if you are using fusible interfacing. Test a piece of fabric first, especially if it is a synthetic.

- Triple-check the sewing machine's tension on a test piece of fabric before you begin the project.

- Change the sewing machine's needle size, if needed, to best suit the material.

Gathers and Ruffles

Begin by stitching a rolled machine hem* (page 154) along one long edge of the fabric piece, and press. Sew two rows of basting stitches at ¼" and ⅜" from the edge, and pull on the bobbin thread to form gathers. Another option is to increase the sewing machine's tension and stitch length at the same time, so the machine gathers the fabric for you as you sew.

But if the machine's tension is finicky, the first option is recommended.

* Some ruffles are made from strips folded in half lengthwise before gathering, so they don't need a hem.

Continuous Bias Trim

I. To create a long, continuous piece of bias tape, begin with a rectangular piece of fabric. Use the following formula to calculate the size of fabric you will need:

   A. Add 12" to the length of bias tape trim you need.

   B. Remove the selvages from the fabric and measure the width. Divide the total from Step A by this measurement.

   C. Multiply the total from Step B by the desired width of the bias tape strips (including seam allowances).

   D. Cut a rectangle the length of the total from Step C × the width of the fabric.

2. Fold down the right-hand corner of the fabric to create a right triangle. Cut along the fold line. With right sides together, align the triangles as shown (Figure 1) and stitch using a ¼" seam allowance. Press open.

3. Using tailor's chalk and a ruler, mark parallel lines spaced the width of the desired bias tape strips (Figure 2).

4. Make a cut approximately 5" deep along the first of the marked lines.

5. Join the 2 sides to form a tube (Figure 3). The raw edge at line A will align with the raw edge at B. This will allow the first line to be offset by a strip width. Pin the raw edges right sides together, making sure that the lines match. Sew with a ¼" seam allowance. Press the seam open.

6. Cut along the drawn lines, creating a continuous strip.

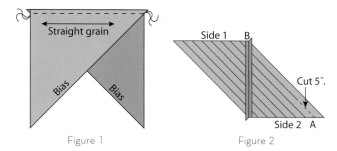

Figure 1

Figure 2

Figure 3

Basic Tablecloths

The ability to sew gives you a wonderful advantage when selecting table linens. You have unlimited options when it comes to sizes, shapes, and colors.

Round Tables

For round tables, we almost always prefer a tablecloth that goes all the way to the floor. It is easy to adapt the projects in this book to fit any table using the chart below.*

Table diameter	Seats	Tablecloth diameter (to the floor)
30"	2–3 people	90"
36"	4–6 people	96"
48"	6 people	108"
60"	8 people	120"
72"	10 people	132"

* Chart assumes tables are the standard height of 30".

Drafting a Large Circle

Lay the fabric on the floor or other flat surface. Cut a piece of twine or heavy string to a length that equals *half* the desired diameter, plus 6" (to attach the string to the chalk). Pin an end of the string to the center of the fabric. Tie the other end of the string to a piece of tailor's chalk, making sure the distance between the center and where the chalk touches the fabric equals half the desired diameter. Carefully mark a circle on the fabric, and cut it out.

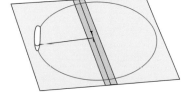

Calculating Ruffles

Adding a ruffle is a simple way to dress up any tablecloth.

For a circular table, use this basic formula to determine how long to cut the strips of fabric for the ruffle:

1. Table diameter + (Table height × 2) = Diameter of tablecloth

2. Tablecloth diameter from Step 1 × 3.15 = Circumference of tablecloth

3. Tablecloth circumference from Step 2 × 1½* = Length of ruffle strips

* For a fuller ruffle, multiply the circumference of the tablecloth by 2 or 3.

Rectangular and Square Tables

For a square or rectangular table, you will want a tablecloth that is square or rectangular in shape. Measure the table top and decide how much of an overhang you would like. Double the overhang measurement and add it to the length of the table to calculate the length of fabric needed. Double the overhang measurement and add it to the width of the tabletop to calculate the width of fabric needed.

RESOURCES

Felt and Fabrics

Andover Fabrics andoverfabrics.com
  *Fabrics (page 126) and
  backdrop (page 131)*

Bella Nonna Quilts bellanonnaquilt.com
  Gold leather (page 77)

C&T Publishing ctpub.com
  *Lutradur and Liquitex paints
  (page 65)*

Michael Miller Fabrics
michaelmillerfabrics.com
  Premade ruffles (page 54)

National Nonwovens
nationalnonwovens.com
  *Felts, including 100% wool and wool/rayon
  blends (throughout the book)*

Robert Kaufman Fabrics
robertkaufman.com
  *Fabrics, including Radiance, Ultra Sateen,
  and Essex linen/cotton blend (throughout
  the book)*

Interfacing

Pellon pellonideas.com
  Interfacing (throughout the book)

Supplies

Hambly Screen Prints hamblyscreenprints.com
  Paper place mats (page 50)

June Tailor Inc. junetailor.com
  *Sew-in computer printer fabric
  (pages 24 and 25)*

Luna Bazaar lunabazaar.com
  Parasols (pages 60 and 61)

Nettleton Hollow nettletonhollow.com
  *Mitsumata branches (page 65)
  (Similar branches can be found at
  Pier 1 Imports.)*

Shinoda Design Center shinodadesigncenter.net
  *Wholesale floral supplies, props, and
  decorations (throughout the book)*

STYROFOAM Brand Foam craftsncoffee.com;
styrofoamcrafts.com
  Polystyrene balls (page 118)

ABOUT
THE AUTHORS

Kelly Lee-Creel is a former video game producer who had a secret crush on fabric design and pattern making. Lots of hard work, much grace, and many adventures later, she is now a licensed fabric designer with Andover Fabrics. She loves fabrics, crafts, decorating, and photography and blogs about it all on her website, everkelly.com. Kelly lives in Seattle with her husband.

Rebecca Söder is a married, stay-at-home mother of two. Her love of baking started when she made Kelly's wedding cake. When people began requesting her specialty cakes and edible creations, she started a small custom cake business right in her kitchen. Right now, Rebecca is busy taking care of her kids and crafting up all sorts of fun projects for her blog, frombeccashome.blogspot.com.

stashBOOKS

fabric arts for a handmade lifestyle

If you're craving beautiful authenticity in a time of mass-production...Stash Books is for you. Stash Books is a line of how-to books celebrating fabric arts for a handmade lifestyle. Backed by C&T Publishing's solid reputation for quality, Stash Books will inspire you with contemporary designs, clear and simple instructions, and engaging photography.

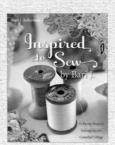

www.stashbooks.com